EXPLORING THE PARABLES

EUGENE S. WEHRLI

AN ADULT RESOURCE BOOK

UNITED CHURCH PRESS

BOSTON • PHILADELPHIA

Contents

CHAPTER

1   *The Puzzling Problem*   5

2   *Nature and Purpose of Parables*   13

3   *The Life Situation*   25

4   *The Parables and the Kingdom*   37

5   *The Kingdom Here and Now*   47

6   *Parables of Crisis*   57

7   *Entering the Kingdom*   69

8   *Relationships of the Kingdom*   85

9   *The Way of God and the Way of Man*   101

10   *Jesus in the Parables*   111

ACKNOWLEDGMENTS   120

APPENDIX:

    Alphabetical Listing of the Parables   122

    Biblical Listing of the Parables   124

And he said, "The kingdom of God is as if a man should scatter seed upon the ground, and should sleep and rise night and day, and the seed should sprout and grow, he knows not how. The earth produces of itself, first the blade, then the ear, then the full grain in the ear. But when the grain is ripe, at once he puts in the sickle, because the harvest has come."

Mark 4: 26–29

Chapter One

THE PUZZLING PROBLEM

"What do you think is the point of this parable in Mark 4:26–29?" asked the leader of the new discussion group in First Church. "How can we find out definitely what Jesus meant to teach his contemporaries?"

John Smythe was first to respond to the leader's probing questions. "I think," he began slowly, "that it means the kingdom of God will grow gradually in our hearts."

"I don't know," contributed Mary Weiss. "I take it to mean that the harvest is God's final judgment on all men."

Cindy Thompson continued the discussion with the suggestion that she thought the seed is the word of God that man is called upon to sow.

"It seems to me," volunteered Henry Elliott, "that it is telling us we can't know God's purpose."

"Oh-h!" muttered Harvey Alden with the glow of an oncoming insight illuminating his whole face. "Might this mean that each of our souls grows inwardly, and can't be taught or tampered with by anyone else?"

Parables are among the most cherished portions of the Scriptures. The simplicity and clarity of their vocabulary and the vividness of the experiences of life pictured in them suggest that parables are simple, straightforward stories which illuminate the general principles or truths of religion. Yet, as the above discussion illustrates, a puzzling problem becomes apparent when we attempt to *interpret* these simple and clear stories—whenever we seek to uncover the Word of God the stories impart.

There is no problem understanding the story of the parable in Mark 4: 26–29. The vocabulary is simple and the incident is a familiar and easily comprehended one. But we have an entirely different situation when we turn to discovering the Word of God this story unfolds. What does it say about the nature of the kingdom of God?

The fact of the matter is that it seems to be easier to *mis*interpret the parables of Jesus than to interpret them correctly. How do you determine whether or not an interpretation is correct? How do you distinguish between interpretations that consist of reading our own ideas into them and those that embody the truths of *God?* How do you differentiate between the voice of God and the opinions of men?

Especially is this a real problem when we turn to a specific way of reading into the parables our own ideas or ideas that Jesus did not intend: allegorizing. Since this is perhaps the most prevalent way of misinterpreting Jesus' parables, it will be instructive, before we explore the nature and purpose of parables, to consider the nature and purpose of allegories, and to contrast the two. This will be significant preparation for our pilgrimage (in later chapters) of actually exploring and interpreting the parables of Christ.

Allegorizing the Parables

An allegory is a make-believe, artificial story in which the characters represent something other than themselves. Often the names themselves indicate that the story is not to be taken at face value. While a parable is an appeal to responsiveness and intelligibility, an allegory can be understood only by those in possession of the key to its system or symbolism. An allegory embodies teaching to be accepted on grounds other than face value, while a parable has the character of an argument laying claim to the insight of the hearer and seeking application to the situation at hand. Willard H. Robinson gives Ruckert's example of an allegory.

> He pictures a man who while falling into a great pit grasps with one hand at the branch of a small tree . . . and saves himself. Below is a dragon waiting to devour him. At the root of the tree are two mice, one white, the other black, incessantly gnawing at the root of the tree. Some luscious berries grow within reach of the man's free hand. These he picks and eats with satisfaction.[1]

This is an artificial story in which quite obviously the real concern is not with the mice and the root. Rather, each is a dimly-veiled symbol for something else. The mice (night and day) gnaw at the root (time) while the dragon (death) waits below. Nevertheless, in his precarious position man enjoys temporary pleasures (berries).

A Classic Example

Almost all of the parables have been read allegorically in periods of the church's history. An interesting example of this is St. Augustine's treatment of the parable of the good Samaritan. It is reported by C. H. Dodd, and it demonstrates that even men prominent in the history of the Christian religion have fallen prey to the temptation to allegorize Jesus' parables.

> A *certain man went down from Jerusalem to Jericho;* Adam himself is meant; *Jerusalem* is the heavenly city of peace, from whose blessedness Adam fell; *Jericho* means the moon, and signifies our mortality, because it is born, waxes, wanes, and dies. *Thieves* are the devil and his angels.*Who stripped him,* namely, of his immortality; *and beat him,* by persuading him to sin; *and left him half-dead,* because in so far as man can understand and know God, he lives, but in so far as he is wasted and oppressed

7

The Good Samaritan

ROGER MART

8

by sin, he is dead; he is therefore called *half-dead*. The *priest* and *Levite* who saw him and passed by, signify the priesthood and ministry of the Old Testament, which could profit nothing for salvation. *Samaritan* means Guardian, and therefore the Lord Himself is signified by this name. The *binding of the wounds* is the restraint of sin. *Oil* is the comfort of good hope; *wine* the exhortation to work with fervent spirit. The *beast* is the flesh in which He deigned to come to us. The being *set upon the beast* is belief in the incarnation of Christ. The *inn* is the Church, where travellers returning to their heavenly country are refreshed after pilgrimage. The *morrow* is after the resurrection of the Lord. The *two pence* are either the two precepts of love, or the promise of this life and of that which is to come. The *innkeeper* is the Apostle (Paul). The supererogatory payment is either his counsel of celibacy, or the fact that he worked with his own hands lest he should be a burden to any of the weaker brethren when the Gospel was new, though it was lawful for him "to live by the Gospel." [2]

I doubt if you have ever thought of this parable in this way. How can we know whether Augustine's interpretation is correct or not? It would be incorrect if this is not what Jesus meant when he told the parable, but how can we find out what Jesus really meant? What are the difficulties of Augustine's interpretation?

To read something allegorically that is not written as such, means that the reader finds things in the story which he already believes. St. Augustine has read his own beliefs into the story of the good Samaritan and reinforced them. While his thoughts reflect the best theology of his time, they have nothing to do with the purpose of Jesus' story.

Getting at the Problem

Look back at the paragraph that opens the book, Mark 4: 26–29. In this parable, the likeness made with the kingdom of God is difficult to determine. We must not let the seed immediately turn our thoughts to the word of God. The discussion is about seed, not a veiled reference to the word of God. Likewise, the harvest mentioned at the end of the parable is a real harvest; not a veiled reference to the last judgment or to anything else. To get at the issue in the parable, let us read the story not as a veiled account of spiritual truth, but as an account of the farming cycle.

What is it about the process from sowing to harvest that Jesus has noted and that he develops in this true-to-life description? The amazing fact is that while the farmer scatters the seed and gathers the harvest, the seed sprout and grow without man's knowing how. The farmer, as the story portrays it, does not create the growth; he merely sleeps and rises night and day. Or as the parable then goes on explicitly to state, "the earth produces of itself." Although man may scatter and gather he is not the instrument of growth. Growth comes apart from the farmer's effort. This is the single significant point of this parable. The message is that the kingdom of God comes apart from human effort and control. We do not create or make it. We may reap its fruits, but in no way are we the cause of them.

As a word of caution let us make sure that we do not read our ideas of farming into the story. The story makes its own point clear. The mention of farming is not permission for us to draw out of the parable any analogy that *we* are likely to make to farming. The parable of the seed growing of itself makes clear the aspect of farming with which Jesus wants to compare the kingdom.

Finally, not every part of the parable has a meaning in relation to the kingdom of God. The parts have their meaning only in relation to the story as a whole and this story, radically different from the kingdom of God, exhibits only *one striking point* of likeness to it. We must read the story in its own terms. Only when this has been done do we dare compare it to the kingdom of God.

10

In proceeding to apply the parable we might say that man must live in trustful dependence upon the heavenly Father. Faith is at the heart of the message—a faith that this is God's world. The harvest does not depend upon the farmer any more than the universe depends upon man. If we could get rid of the obsession that all depends upon us, we would be free to do our own work without anxiety, knowing that God is over all and that the increase comes from him. Concern over success or failure would not oppress us and, as the farmer, we would rise and sleep in confidence while God accomplished his purpose (we knowing not how). Such confidence would enable us to do our work without anxiety about success or about what we would accomplish. It is tremendously moving and profoundly true that God is the Ruler; his kingdom is at work, even while we are sleeping.

We seek security in feverish activity. We always want to know what we can do. When there is something we can do, we feel in control—master of the situation.

People often hold the attitude, "Nobody can help me. I must make myself more appealing, a better student, more friendly." But such striving only leads to greater agony and self-reproval. Our struggling soul must finally realize that it is dependent. There is help that can come from without. A psychiatrist's patient may discover this fact by experiencing the help of the counselor upon whom he is dependent. But if healing is to be permanent for any of us, we must finally surrender ourselves to dependence upon God.

Because such dependence is so easy to deny, the puzzling problem—an eternal one—is: How do we get at the parables of Jesus in such a way as to perceive the Word of God rather than the opinions of men?

And when he was alone, those who were about him with the twelve asked him concerning the parables. And he said to them, "To you has been given the secret of the kingdom of God, but for those outside everything is in parables; so that they may indeed see but not perceive, and may indeed hear but not understand; lest they should turn again, and be forgiven." Mark 4: 10–12

"This is why I speak to them in parables, because seeing they do not see, and hearing they do not hear, nor do they understand." Matthew 13: 13

Chapter Two

NATURE AND PURPOSE OF PARABLES

If a parable is not an allegory, what is it?

The word *parable* is Greek (*parabole*), and denotes a comparison or analogy. The Old Testament way of putting it is "to be like," from the Hebrew word, *mashal*. (See Job 41: 33.) It is, in this sense, a comparison of the familiar with the strange, of the clearly-understood with the more veiled. It draws illustrations from daily life in order to impart the Word of God.

Actually, parables are frequently constructed in our own day. Many times we are in the position where we cannot explain something except to say, "It is like . . ." When we do this we usually continue with a picture or story of something that we consider to be as familiar as possible to our hearer and that will compare this familiar object or idea with the less apparent one that we wish to illuminate.

Jesus' parables have their roots in the riddles, analogies, vivid comparisons, and pithy sayings of the Old Testament. More than anything else they owe their existence to the illuminating figures of speech that were so characteristic of the language of the Hebrew people of Jesus' day. These gave rise to comparisons and analogies, containing metaphors, that went beyond single words to word pictures and illuminating stories.

Isaiah gives us two analogies, both comparing familiar features of farming with less apparent realities. In the first (Isaiah 28: 23–26) he points out that plowing is a temporary procedure. Its purpose is not to beat the ground, but to prepare it for the sowing of the seed. The analogy is to God's judgment. God does not "plow" his people for the sake of destroying them; his purpose is to prepare them to be fruitful in doing his will.

The second analogy (Isaiah 28: 27–29) takes its image from threshing rather than plowing. The analogy points out that the farmer uses various methods of threshing, depending upon the nature of the grain. If he is not careful, the fine grain is crushed by too-heavy sledges. On the other hand, coarse grain may not be threshed if his instrument is too delicate. Furthermore, no one threshes forever, but solely to separate the grain from the chaff. Similarly, God does not judge to destroy, but to purify; and he, too, uses a method that takes account of the condition of his people.

Jeremiah makes extensive use of parables that are really analogous stories. The parable of the potter (Jeremiah 18: 1–12) is based upon Jeremiah's observation of the potter's technique when a vessel on his wheel is spoiled. When the potter is dissatisfied he returns the clay into the lump and remolds the vessel. Jeremiah makes the analogy between the way that the potter works and the working of God, who, if his people do not fulfill his intent, can start over with a new people of his own choosing. Israel is dependent upon God, not he upon them. The parables of Jeremiah are analogies pointing to a likeness between radically different subjects.

Locating the Parables in the New Testament

When we turn to the New Testament armed with such an understanding of the definition and antecedents of the parables of Jesus, we discover that it is still exceedingly difficult to decide just which passages of the Scriptures are parables. The term "parable" is applied to many different portions of the Bible by writers of the New Testament.

The name parable is sometimes applied to *proverbial sayings,* as in Mark 7: 15: "There is nothing outside a man which by going into him can defile him; but the things which come out of a man are what defile him," and in Mark 3: 24: "If a kingdom is divided against itself that kingdom cannot stand." But the Gospels do not always state which of their passages are parables. Closely related to and hard to distinguish from parables are *proverbs.* A proverb is a condensation of human experience, usually using concrete analogies to convey its message. The sentence, "Physician, heal yourself" (Luke 4: 23), is referred to as a proverb in the Scriptures. On the other hand the word parable is sometimes translated *lesson,* "From the fig tree learn its lesson" in Mark 13: 28. (See also Matthew 24: 32.) Thus, the word parable can refer to proverbial sayings; or, since a proverb is a maxim that has been distilled out of human experience, the word can occasionally be used to refer to the meaning of that experience—its lesson.

The most important New Testament usage of the word parable grows out of the use of *metaphors* and *similes* in concrete speech. It is often difficult to tell where a metaphor or simile ceases to be and a parable exists. A metaphor or simile involves a single word or a small group of words—a figure of speech—for comparison, whereas *a parable usually designates a narrative or describes a process in which there is some comparison.* This is the common usage of the word parable today.

A few stories that are commonly referred to as parables are really *illustrative stories* and are not extended metaphors at all. Such stories, which provide examples for human behavior, can end with the message, "Go thou and do likewise"— a remark highly inappropriate to the metaphorical story.

Because of the variety of meanings attached to the term parable, scholars differ on the number of passages of the Scriptures that are to be called parables. Some of the differences between the scholars are occasioned by differences in the Gospels themselves. Where one Gospel uses the term parable to indicate a teaching, a comparable Gospel uses no such term. Gospel writers made no attempt to point out all parables, and so parables must be identified on the basis of similarity to named ones and upon an understanding of their characteristics and features.

Techniques of Oral Communication

Our understanding of the parables is enhanced if we bear in mind that they were originally a form of oral communication. Though they come to us in written form, Jesus told them, informally, to various audiences.

These oral stories are realistic descriptions, true-to-life and complete in themselves. Each object stands for itself alone and is not a symbol of something else. If, for example, a parable is about a farmer and his crops, it will give a clear and meaningful—as well as accurate—account of farm life. If the parable is about a shepherd and his sheep, it will contain a true-to-life description of pastoral life. Even a parable that has an imaginative setting, such as the parable of the rich man and Lazarus (see Luke 16: 19–31), is realistic in manner and contains true-to-life conversation.

Over long centuries, storytellers found that there are special tricks of the trade, so to speak, that impart heightened effectiveness to their stories. When Jesus told his true-to-life stories, he employed some of these time-honored techniques of oral communication. In *Interpreting the Parables,* Archibald M. Hunter deals with the first four of the following techniques of oral communication employed by Jesus in the telling of the parables.[1]

16

PARABLES USE REPETITION. This is a technique that helps us to remember the stories of the parables. Examples are the parable of the talents and the parable of the foundations.

CONTRAST IS USED TO MAKE VIVID THE DECISIVE POINT. The good Samaritan is contrasted with the priest and the Levite, Lazarus with the rich man, the Pharisee with the publican, the prodigal with the elder brother, and the wise maidens with the foolish ones.

THE ORAL STORY OFTEN USES THE RULE OF THREE. It is cast in a threefold form. Again memory is abetted, and dramatic effect is heightened. The fruitless seed falls on three kinds of soil, while the fruitful seed produces in three amounts in the parable of the sower. There are three travelers on the road to Jericho in the parable of the good Samaritan. The rule of three is also used in other forms of literature as, for example, in the children's stories, "The Three Bears" and "The Three Little Pigs."

THE PARABLE OFTEN EMPLOYS THE DEVICE OF END STRESS. Emphasis falls on the final act of the story. Preliminary remarks only set the stage for concluding ones. The vineyardist sent out his son after the servants were repeatedly rejected. Stress falls on the good Samaritan and on the man who buried his talent.

ORAL STORIES OFTEN ARE CHARACTERIZED BY AN ECONOMY OF WORDS. The parables vary considerably in length, but no matter what their length they do not spin out the story for the story's sake.

The quality of some of this narrative as narrative is often overlooked. It was a teacher of English literature and not a professor of Bible who pointed out to me many years ago the bare narrative quality of many of the finest parables. If you will take as an example the parable of the prodigal son and eliminate all descriptive adjectives and adverbs, all description of any kind, you will take almost nothing from the story. It is action itself in words. It is narrative stripped to the running gears, without adornment and without refinement.[2]

Functional Features

While the parables of Jesus make use of special techniques of oral communication, they also contain functional features that help us to understand why Jesus chose to utilize them as a vehicle for his teaching.

COMPARING THE ESSENTIALLY UNLIKE

A parable gains its force by comparing things that are essentially unlike. Who would guess that there was any likeness between the story of the mustard seed and the kingdom of God? Yet when you discover this astounding and unexpected likeness, the point of the parable is driven home. Jesus continually uses unusual comparison and exaggeration to shock his listeners with the truth that cuts into their self-righteousness. It is the dissimilarity of the things compared that makes the meaning of the parables become startling, clear, and vivid.

Let's try to illustrate this by using a metaphor. A young lover says to his girl, "You're a peach!" Here two unlike things are compared. Who would ever guess that there could be any likeness between a girl and a peach? Because we use this figure of speech so often it has become trite and doesn't demand much thought beyond the implied comparison of sweetness. But if the girl were a foreigner and heard the saying for the first time, she might wonder, "Did he mean that I have a stony heart, or that I have a fuzzy skin?" But when the true likeness is discerned it is driven home with force, since all other aspects of the things compared are so radically unlike.

18

Remember that in a parable the comparison is with the whole process that the story describes and not with any single object of the story. When it is said in Matthew 13: 31 that "the kingdom of heaven is like a grain of mustard seed which . . ." the kingdom of God is not being compared to a mustard seed but to the surprising likeness between the kingdom and the whole process of the mustard seed's becoming a plant. The introduction might be paraphrased to suggest this by the words, "The case of the kingdom of God is like the case of the mustard seed which . . ."

AN APPEAL TO OUR INSIGHT

Parables appeal to our insight. They demand understanding and responsiveness. The fact that the comparison is concealed, and that the demand to understand is implicit in the story, causes us to seek, grasp, and snap at the meaning. The form of parables demands reflection and participation. If the illustrative metaphor were, "Your face is an autumn moon," struggle would be necessary to grasp the meaning. Yet when the true comparison is found, it is easily remembered because we arrived at it through active personal struggle with a vivid and memorable figure of speech.

The power of the parables to arouse insight is achieved through their vivid visual appeal. A parable entices the imagination with a striking word picture. It presents "a truth so *substantial* that it feeds imagination and does not merely outline an idea. It was that way of conceiving reality which was always characteristic of the Hebrew mind."[3]

In their appeal to the imagination parables bring to the surface what might have been ambiguously or hazily felt beforehand. What was half known is now clearly seen. Parables call to light what is veiled or only dimly felt. In doing so, they separate the wheat from the chaff, the true from the questionable. They reveal thought more perfectly to those of us who understand, and hide it from those of us who do not.

Extensive use of questions forces us to make decisions that involve us in the recognition of correct choices. This also aids in clarifying otherwise unclear concepts. Some parables even begin with a question, as in the two sons: "What do you think?" (Matthew 21:28). Others end with one, as in the good Samaritan: "Which of these three . . . proved neighbor?" (Luke 10:36) and in the two debtors, "Now which of them will love him more?" (Luke 7:42). The parable has made the answer to the question so clear that we cannot help but know the correct answer.

ACTIVE INVOLVEMENT

The Old Testament illustrates that parables are a means of actively involving us and of inevitably driving home their meaning when our guard is down. By enticing us to pursue their veiled meanings while we are still unaware of all that is involved, the parables infiltrate our lives with their messages—even though we would have rejected or refused to listen to them if we had foreseen what would happen.

After David had murdered Uriah and married Bathsheba the prophet Nathan confronted him with a story (see 2 Samuel 12:1–4) in which a wealthy man wronged a poor man by taking his one precious possession. When David heard the story his fairness as a judge blazed forth with the words, "The man who has done this deserves to die" (2 Samuel 12:5). By means of this objective story Nathan had acted so that David pronounced justly, and it was easy for Nathan to say, "You are the man," (2 Samuel 12:7). In discovering the justness of the judgment in the story, David discovered his own status before God.

Parables judge us by revealing us to ourselves. By their comparisons parables conceal their meanings, challenging us to unravel the meanings for ourselves. By the time we find the meaning of a parable, that meaning is already established in our mind and it is too late to guard against finding it.

Clarity comes only when the stimulating demand of a parable is met by our activity. A parable is understood only by him who has eyes to see, ears to hear. To penetrate it, we must grasp at it with both mind and heart. By the time we discover its truth, we have been captured. The power and the words stick like irritating burrs. They cut through previous religious platitudes and previous conceptions.

The Purpose of the Parables

The most puzzling statement about the purpose of the parables is in Mark 4: 11–12: "To you has been given the secret of the kingdom of God, but for those outside everything is in parables; so that they may indeed see but not perceive, and may indeed hear but not understand; lest they should turn again, and be forgiven." These verses stress the idea that a parable imparts God's Word only for the person who grasps for its meaning in faith. A parable is not a shortcut that enables one to get the answers without the insight and the discipline of faith.

Yet these verses in Mark are difficult because they seem to imply that God conceals, not so that the person who would understand must grasp for meaning, but so that God might keep people from knowing the secret of his kingdom. The important thing to note is that these are verses written in retrospect by an author who was apparently looking back and reflecting upon the functioning of the parables in the lives of the people in whose midst he had lived. What he observed, in retrospect, was the fact that those persons who had remained outside of active involvement in the kingdom were outside because they did not perceive the parable's meaning with the eye of faith. "Seeing they do not see" Matthew 13: 13). What was indeed a fact or consequence— that not all responded favorably—was seen in retrospect as the purpose of the parables.

21

The purpose or major function of the parables is *to impart the Word of God to man so that he responds: this response may take either a positive or a negative form.* To be sure, such an imparting of God's Word is concealed by a superficial study of the parables. We must work hard to grasp the meaning Jesus conveyed in the parables. On the other hand, when we take them seriously they push us either to one side or to the other side of the fence of neutrality and luke-warmness.

Such an interpretation of the purpose of the parables, based on Mark 4: 11-12, appears meaningful both by comparison with the other Gospels and by studying the words in Greek, which was their original language. The form of the parables becomes a judgment upon us when we look at the words as they are in Matthew 13: 13, 16: "This is why I speak to them in parables, because seeing they do not see, and hearing they do not hear, nor do they understand. . . . But blessed are your eyes, for they see, and your ears, for they hear." The form either reveals our hardness of heart and our spiritual dullness or it communicates a blessing upon us if we can truly see and hear. This meaning is clearly indicated in Matthew 13: 12: "For to him who has will more be given, and he will have abundance; but from him who has not, even what he has will be taken away." Luke 8: 18 prefaces this remark with the injunction, "Take heed then how you hear," indicating that it was understood to refer to the responsibility of comprehending the words of Jesus. (See also Mark 4: 25.)

Matthew connects the whole interpretation with Isaiah's description of his own mission. It is typical for Matthew to relate the words to the Old Testament. As Isaiah looked at his ministry in retrospect he saw that the true consequence of his prophetic preaching had not been merely to save, but rather he had separated the spiritually discerning from the undiscerning through the way people had responded to his message. (Compare Luke 10: 16: "He who hears you hears me, and he who rejects you rejects me.") The total effect of the parables is *to hold us responsible for hearing.*

Joachim Jeremias, in explaining the form of the statement in Mark 4: 1–11 not only finds in its vocabulary evidence of the originality of the statement, but in trying to get the force of the saying in the original language comments that it is clear that the word translated *parables* here implies, not the parables as we designate them, but the Hebrew sense of the word *riddles.* Those outside are confronted by riddles—they cannot discern the sense of it.[4] Thus we see that the parables not only demand a response to their message but that we are judged by the response which we give. Not to discern is to see riddles. The purpose of the parables is not to keep us from being forgiven; but we do reveal our own receptivity by our response to the parables. When we are not receptive we cut ourselves off from forgiveness.

The parables must never be thought of as mere sermon illustrations stating in picture form some general truths. They are the Word of God, quick and powerful and sharper than any two-edged sword, piercing and penetrating. Their effectiveness is not in their illustration; instead, it is in our responsiveness.

So he told them this parable: "What man of you, having a hundred sheep, if he has lost one of them, does not leave the ninety-nine in the wilderness, and go after the one which is lost, until he finds it? And when he has found it, he lays it on his shoulders, rejoicing. And when he comes home, he calls together his friends and his neighbors, saying to them, 'Rejoice with me, for I have found my sheep which was lost.' Even so, I tell you, there will be more joy in heaven over one sinner who repents than over ninety-nine righteous persons who need no repentance." Luke 15: 3–7

Chapter Three

THE LIFE SITUATION

The teaching of Jesus was not formally delivered to massed audiences of passive listeners. His teaching was given in response to questions put to him, through comments on things and events about him, by apt explanations related to the audience at hand. The fact that it grew out of the life situation in which Jesus and the disciples were involved made the teaching of Jesus relevant to the times and the lives of those who heard him. Both subject matter and application of the parables relate directly to life's problems. Rather than stories illustrating eternal religious truths or ideas, the parables set forth the purpose of God as it is related to specific situations. It is the particularity of the parables that gives them their challenge and judging power.

The Need for Reapplication

As the church told the parables through the succeeding years, however, their application to life was often altered or forgotten. As we read the parables today, we apply them to situations different from those Jesus saw as he went about Galilee. To apply the parables of Jesus to a situation different from that which the first century faced is perfectly legitimate, if it is the central and original meaning of the parable that is applied. The original purpose of Jesus' teaching is fulfilled only to the extent that it is made relevant to the specific issues of the time in which we live. Application of the basic meaning is always the end product of interpretation.

The necessity for applying the meaning of a given parable to the issue at hand is evident in the Gospels themselves. Different Gospels apply the same parables to different situations. Obviously, in their early usage the parables were seen to be relevant to the everyday problems of life, and one parable was applied to a variety of problems. The Gospel of Matthew, which was written about fifty years after the death of Jesus, is clearly composed with the recognition that the teaching of Jesus speaks to the problems of the early church, and shows how some parables apply to the life of the church around 80 A.D. Luke, on the other hand, indicates a widely divergent application of the same parables.

Several results occurred in this dynamic treatment of the parables. One is that *the original situation was often neglected in the written Gospels because the times had changed and the central truths of the parables did not demand the recording of particular applications in order to discern their meaning.* In such cases the parables give their meaning without specific indication of the group or situation to which they were originally addressed.

Another result is that *the evangelists sometimes have preserved an indication of the intended application of the parable.* Often the application is so integral to the parable itself that no separation of the two has been made. The parable of the children in the marketplace, for example, has its original application to the kind of reception that Jesus and John the Baptist were accorded by the people (see Matthew 11: 16); the two debtors applies to Simon the Pharisee (see Luke 7: 36–50).

A third result is that *often two of the evangelists have made different applications of the same parable.* What has most likely happened in these instances is that one of the evangelists, at least, seeking to make clear the relevance of the teaching of Jesus to the problems of a later day and a different people, has set forth clearly the new application of the parable. If one examines the parables in their context in the Gospels, it becomes evident that the evangelists treated the settings and the applications of the parables much more freely than the parables themselves. In this the evangelists were good preachers, always making the words of Jesus relevant to the lives of their listeners. Thus the parables were prevented from becoming mere pious talk.

VARIOUS APPLICATIONS OF THE PARABLE OF THE LOST SHEEP

An example of different applications of the same parable is found in the parable of the lost sheep (see Luke 15: 3–7 and Matthew 18: 12–14). In Luke the parable is told to the Pharisees and scribes in answer to their criticism, "This man receives sinners and eats with them." Applied to the Pharisees the parable portrays the eager searching of God for even one of his lost ones, and his joy when the recovery takes place. This way of God is in contrast to the Pharisees' squeamish holiness. In confronting the self-righteous who are critical of association with sinners, the parable shows God's concern for sinners—the lost. It makes its point by appealing to a common practice of those addressed. Would they not search for the lost sheep, and rejoice when it was found? So also God rejoices over one sinner who repents.

Let us put the message of the parable in other words: "So you would protect your holiness by avoiding outcasts and the disreputable person in society? Purity to you means not to associate with or touch anything impure. Holiness is to avoid bad company. Well, not so with God. God's holiness leads him to seek to associate with the immoral and the dissolute. Purity means to seek to save what is lost. Holiness is seen in aggressive love. He does not withdraw from the evil one, but seeks to recover what is lost. Holiness is not measured by chastity or abstinence, but by a seeking love. God's way differs from yours. In your very criticism, however hostile you may be, you have seen how God acts."

27

*Every person, no matter how insignificant
in the world's eyes, is precious to God*

Such an application of the parable has many ramifications that we could try to develop if we were expressing our personal feelings. "We are numbered among the murmurers, critical of a God who is so unrealistically good, forgiving terrible men. There are some people whom we just cannot— nay, must not—deal with in good faith. If we deal with them they get the better of us, and often corrupt us. God, your way is good, but not pertinent to or realistic when dealing with communists. Your way cannot be used to deal with the social and moral issues of our day."

In such an application we would be numbered among the self-righteous and the respectable. God's ways would seem to be ridiculous and would be criticized by us as well as by the Pharisees. The parable says, "You are right. You have discerned that God's ways are not your ways. Your calculations do not fit God's goodness. His love and your fear of being taken advantage of make sharp contrasts. You are miles apart from God."

The setting given to the parable of the lost sheep in Matthew is different, and consequently the application takes a radically altered form. Here the parable is addressed to the faithful disciples rather than to the self-righteous critics of God's lavish goodness. When addressed to the faithful disciples the same parable sounds something like this: "God seeks out the lost sheep and rejoices when it is found. He goes to unending lengths to recover what is lost. What meaning does this have for you disciples? It means that you, too, as faithful servants of God, must seek out the lost in our world as diligently as does your heavenly Father. The implications of this are really twofold:

1. "See that you do not despise one of these little ones. Every single person, no matter how insignificant in the world's eyes, is precious to God. Therefore, you must not despise any of them."

2. "It is not the will of my Father that one of these little

ones should perish. You must, therefore, seek the lost, for that is the will and the work of your Father in heaven. You must be missionary-minded toward all men because all are precious to the Father. No one must perish; and you must, as your Father in heaven, search for the one that has gone astray—or who has never known or heard the Father."

Here we see an application made to the disciples as faithful followers who are to be like their Father in heaven. This kind of setting is typical for Matthew who has written a Gospel for the life and discipline of the early church and interprets the teaching of Jesus in relation to the problems faced by the church. Those sayings of Jesus that originally applied to the Pharisees must now be understood as they relate to disciples.

There is a third application which can be made by the modern preacher that is just as relevant to the point of the parable, even though it is not made in the Bible at all in connection with this parable. It is the application to the remorseful and self-castigating sinner:

"So you have discovered your sin against God, and have lost all hope. You have betrayed your Master like a Judas, and now the horrible recognition of this has come home to you. You despair. But wait! The Father is a God of seeking love. This is what the parable says, for God is such a God that he takes the lost sheep back into the fold. Nay, even more than that, you would never have discovered your sin and distance from him had he not come to you first and revealed your wickedness by making you aware of your distance from him. It was only when God had come close enough to you in your wandering plight that you recognized the seriousness of your condition. Even your despair, therefore, is an indication of God's closeness to you and of his seeking you when you were farthest from him. Know his love, humble yourself by grasping it, and hold onto the everlasting rock.

"Do not be foolish and believe that there is something

30

you must first do to be worthy of his love. Do not seek to punish yourself with penance and self-discipline so that you will feel worthy. Such a thought only means that you are still proud and believe in saving yourself. To such men the Savior sent from God means nothing. Would you presume to be so arrogant as to nullify God's salvation by saving yourself through penance and other forms of self-inflicted punishment so that you would make yourself worthy of God and thereby nullify his love? Rejoice rather, for God has already found you and he is rejoicing. You are already his and you will have his peace if you accept him."

Many Applications from One Basic Point

In each of these applications, two of which are made in the biblical text, and a third which is not, the same central point of the story is set forth—God's seeking after the lost. Different applications must always set forth the *one basic point* of the parable. They are not a license to read into the parable ideas that are not found within it, nor is it permissible to dwell on different details of the story. However, a variety of applications to all conditions of men does arise from a single parable. The three applications here vary because of the different people to whom the parable is addressed. The application by Luke, and probably that which Jesus made when he told the parable, is to the self-righteous. The application made by Matthew is to the disciples. The third is to the distraught sinner.

Notice that the parable has relevance to us because we, the hearers, are all of these things often at the same time—most of the time. We are self-righteous, condemning the impurity of others; we are disciples seeking to serve the heavenly Father; and we are distraught sinners aware and fearful of the fact that there is no health in us. On any specific occasion one of these facets needs to be stressed more urgently than any other. The parable fulfills its purpose only when applied to the situation in which we are.

TWO USES OF THE PARABLE OF THE DEFENDANT

The parable of the defendant is likewise found in two different settings in Luke and Matthew. In Luke 12: 57–59 the crowd is the target of the saying of Jesus. He is admonishing the dull crowd that cannot discern the ways of God among men for its failure to understand the seriousness of the times. (See Luke 12: 56.) So the hearer is about to stand before God the Judge, and he must settle before time runs out. The parable runs: "When are you going to be able to discern between right and wrong? You must learn to judge what is right; for if you do not, your case will be turned over to the magistrate and it will be too late for you to have anything to say. Strict justice will have to run its course. Therefore, if you realize how soon you might lose jurisdiction over your case, you will settle with the accuser before justice must take its course. Judgment before God is imminent. You are already on the way to court. Settle your affairs before time runs out. For when you drag one another to court to satisfy your selfish wills, you will discover that you are on trial before *God*. You are bound to lose in this court. You are not in a position where you can demand your 'rights,' but where you must learn to judge what is right."

In Matthew 5: 23–26 the parable is part of the Sermon on the Mount. The subject is the necessity of being at peace with your brother. The context is not in judging what is right, but it is: "So if you are offering your gift at the altar, and there remember that your brother has something against you, leave your gift there before the altar and go; first be reconciled to your brother, and then come and offer your gift." The injunction is, "Make friends quickly with your accuser." The disciple must go to all lengths to be reconciled to his brother. The application is not to the dull crowd but to fellow members in the church. "Be reconciled to your brother." Here the parable applies to conduct toward your neighbor rather than reminding you of the ultimate Judge before whom you must soon stand. This application puts emphasis on the crucial nature of relationships in the church's life. Failure to achieve these relationships means to stand in judgment. Here again Matthew has the church in mind, directing the saying of Jesus toward the disciples.

Trends in Reapplication

Most of the parables of Jesus that were addressed to the multitude or to his opponents had to be reapplied in order to become relevant for the disciples and members of the early church. Furthermore, since the Gospels were written out of the life of the church, and for the use of the church, it was necessary that this process of reapplication take place in the very message of the Gospels themselves.

As we have shown previously, the early church discovered that the same parable has implications for many situations. The gospel writers were not legalists adhering to the original setting. The good news of God was universal and therefore relevant to every new setting in life, and the evangelists sought to make this clear. It is this same conviction that leads us to apply parables to the behavior of people in the twentieth century. In interpreting a parable it is important that we know (1) its central idea and (2) the identity of the original hearers. What meaning did it have for the original hearers? Only when these issues are understood can the parable be safely applied to another problem in another age. To fail to consider both of these factors means in many cases to read our own ideas into the Bible, rather than to let the Bible speak to us.

We have observed that the parables of Jesus often are found in two contexts in the biblical materials. First, they were given by Jesus to the crowds or to his opponents. Next, they were applied in Christian exhortation and Christian education to the training and nurture of disciples in the church. This makes it possible for us to relate the teaching of Jesus to our own day. There are a number of parables and sayings of Jesus that are not given in two forms and addressed to two different groups which, nevertheless, as they are given in the gospel, are clearly applied to a later situation faced by the church.

On several occasions the parables of the crisis of the kingdom breaking in are reapplied by the church to deal with the second coming of Christ. The parable of the ten maidens, most likely told to suggest the closeness of God and his kingdom, is applied to the second coming. In Matthew the parable of the talents deals with the crucial responsibility of the disciple in the light of the imminent coming of the King of all. It has been said that this parable was told in Luke in order to discourage those who thought the kingdom was coming soon. It is used to account for the delay in the second coming. The parable about the wedding garment, joined to the parable of the invitation to the feast in Matthew (not in Luke), is applied to those gathered in the church who are not members in good standing.

Often a parable is concluded with some general remarks that were not part of the original setting of the parable but which to the evangelist summarize in general fashion, in the way that Jesus did, the theme of the parable. Frequently, these generalized sayings of Jesus are given in a number of places, suggesting that the church used them as favorite slogans. These sayings are at best on related subjects and are not the point of the parable. For example, the parable of the dishonest steward in Luke 16: 1–8 is used as the occasion for introducing a number of statements on wealth. (Compare Luke 16: 9–13.) These statements are gathered here because they pertain to the same subject as that of the parable.

Allegorical interpretations are found at the end of a few parables like the sower. If these were told as parables and not allegories, as the form would seem to suggest, the allegorical application would seem to give an early Christian sermon on a situation faced by the church.

Thought Context in the Gospel

We have been illustrating how the single point of a parable might have several applications depending on the nature of the group addressed. It is also important in interpreting a parable of Jesus to understand the context given it in the gospel in order to determine its central message. For example, in the story of the barren fig tree (see Luke 13: 6–9) it would be possible to read it as an indication that God is always willing to give man another chance. The impetuous owner wants to destroy the fruitless vine, but the vinedresser pleads for another chance for the vine to be fruitful and then gives it the best care.

Such an interpretation of the parable ignores the context in which the Gospel according to Luke places it. The parable follows and illuminates, in Luke's understanding of it, the phrase, "Unless you repent, you will all likewise perish" (Luke 13: 5). The story proclaims that the decisive hour for obeying God has come, even as the vine is under judgment by the owner and faces the owner's final decision. It is not divine love but the urgency that God's presence gives to life that is at issue here. The context makes clear that this is not a threat of doomsday or condemnation, but a call to repentance. A survey of what precedes or follows the parable in the text often gives a clue to the meaning intended by the writer.

"No one sews a piece of unshrunk cloth on an old garment; if he does, the patch tears away from it, the new from the old, and a worse tear is made. And no one puts new wine into old wineskins; if he does, the wine will burst the skins, and the wine is lost, and so are the skins; but new wine is for fresh skins."

Mark 2: 21–22

Chapter Four

THE PARABLES AND THE KINGDOM

The kingdom of God is central in Jesus' teaching. The largest number of parables deal with it. The kingdom does not designate a place, a geographical location on a map. Neither is it a reference to the future life. Rather, it designates God's rule.

In Greek, the noun *kingdom* is made out of a verb. It therefore carries with it more of the idea of action than our English words "king" and "kingdom." These words are static, designating things or places, since we do not have an English verb, "to king." A more comparable English word to suggest something of the activity implied in the Greek is our noun *rule* or *rulership,* which comes from the active verb *to rule.* Hence, if we talk of the rule of God, or even of the sovereignty of God, we get a more accurate English equivalent of the original Greek word. We must always remember that the phrase "kingdom of God" does not imply place or geographical location as much as it suggests the active rule of God—his Kingship. Nor does kingdom designate a condition within men or an ideal order of nations; instead, it focuses on the person who rules. Where God rules, we might say, the kingdom is.

The use of the term *kingdom of heaven* in Matthew needs an explanation. Often where Mark uses the phrase "kingdom of God," Matthew uses "kingdom of heaven." Matthew seems to continue, as did the Jews of his day, to refrain from using the personal name for God, since the deity was considered too holy to be referred to intimately by sinful human lips. Hence, *heaven* is a general and impersonal substitute for the personal name God.

THE LABORERS IN THE VINEYARD

What are the content ideas of the kingdom of God? In Matthew 20: 1–16, the kingdom is likened to the reckoning of laborers. The arresting thing is the unusual method of paying the workers. All of them receive the same wage regardless of when they were employed. This is the point in which the comparison to the rule of God exists. The householder had every right to give to the last employed as he gave to the first, by agreement. So the kingdom is God's to give freely as he sees fit, for it belongs to him. "I choose to give to this last as I give to you. Am I not allowed to do what I choose with what belongs to me?" (Matthew 20: 14–15). The kingdom is God's, not man's.

But this leads to grumbling on the part of the laborers, and in this reaction lies the realism of the story. So the parable really contains a rebuke for those who begrudge God's generous and lavish giving. "Do you begrudge my generosity?" God chooses to give his gifts freely, even to the undeserving; but man resents such prominence and prestige bestowed on those who do not deserve it—unless he himself is the recipient of it. Comparison leads to jealousy and resentment. Helmut Thielicke comments on these matters in *The Waiting Father:*

> The long-term workers in the parable would certainly have had no quarrel with the householder's generosity if they themselves had enjoyed the benefit of it. . . . All of us every now and then send up our thanks to heaven when we feel that a hand of blessing has touched our lives, when we get a promotion in our job or when a child comes into our life. Everybody says "Thank God" when some success or other is granted to him. Oh, no, we are not ungrateful. . . .

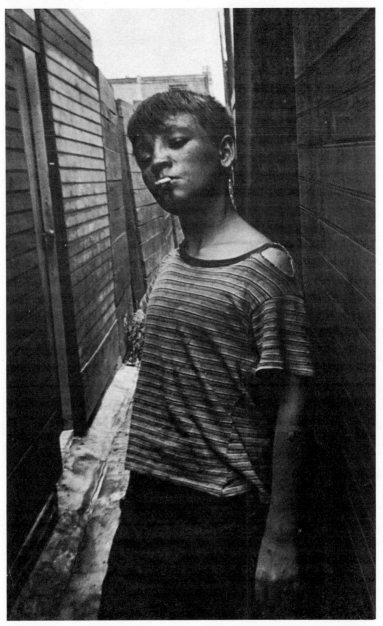

*God's recreating love is lavished with equal fervor
on all manner of his children*

But when I see God giving something out of the ordinary to my competitor, my colleague, perhaps even to my friend, I get sore and begin to check up on the way the various quotas of blessings are handed out and distributed.

When God in his goodness hands out bonuses to *others* and I grow jealous, I do not normally reproach myself and call myself a miserable grudger. (No, we don't say anything like that to ourselves. After all, one has to be a little bit nice to oneself; a man mustn't lose his self-regard.) Nor do I say: O the generosity, the boundless goodness of God! (For this I say only when the Care Package is delivered at my door.) What I say is that this goodness of God is unjust. . . .

God's goodness comes to the wrong person because it doesn't come to me.[1]

Certainly, as a business practice such action is patently unjust, but God's working and bestowing is not a matter of business calculation. The business point of view of the laborers and their offense portrays vividly that God's relations to men are not based on financial figuring. God's doing is not based on human standards of measurement. Men do not earn God's favor. In business men would be offended by such procedure, but this is just how God does—he gives lavishly. The calculating jealousy of the workers who labored during the heat of the day parallels closely the jealousy of the elder brother when the father kills the fatted calf for the prodigal son. The parable stresses God's generous and free-giving of what belongs to him, and rebukes the grudging attitude of those who resent God's goodness as it is shown to the undeserving.

THINGS THIS PARABLE DOES NOT TEACH

Let us now try to clarify several side issues. The parable does not teach that it is never too late to repent. The laborers are not symbols or allegories of repentant people. Furthermore, the parable makes nothing of the idea that it is ever too late to begin work. The laborers are the recipients of an action, not the initiators of it. Neither is the parable an analogy for employer-employee relationships as if it were trying to picture the ideal business behavior.

The central point might have some consequences for understanding both repentance and business practices, but it does not set forth the ideal form of either. If God gives freely of what is his, rather than on the basis of merit, then it is possible that anyone might receive of this generosity regardless of his previous behavior. Also, there is a higher relation than business relations and merited earnings that binds men together. Neither of these can ever heal the wounds of society, and they always remind men of the incapacity of economic activity to save society.

The kingdom is a gift of God's choosing, and he dispenses it without concern for man's sense of values as regards payment, obligation, or dessert. When man objects to the danger of such lavishness, God demands the right to do as he wills with what is his. He does not have to conform to man's puny concept of self-prestige and merit. His kingdom is something he gives, not what man earns.

Verse 16 of Matthew 20 obviously is a case where a well-known saying of Jesus has been appended. This parable does not try to say the last will be first. It is an accidental feature of the story that the last hired are first paid. It is only a device in the story, setting the stage for the disgust of those that worked all day. Actually this statement fits other situations more acceptably. (See Matthew 19: 30; Luke 13: 30.)

INVITATION TO THE BANQUET (MARRIAGE FEAST)

In Luke 14: 15–24 and in Matthew 22: 1–10 we have a parable closely related to the laborers in the vineyard. Here the kingdom is compared to the story of a wedding feast. A man sent out invitations to a great banquet, but those invited did not come. So he extended the invitation to others—the poor, the lame, the blind, the maimed. His servants gathered all whom they found, so that the banquet hall was filled with guests. Matthew's record says that the servants gathered all whom they found, "both good and bad." Both versions suggest that the invitation is freely extended regardless of the condition of the recipient.

A comparison of the account of Luke with that in Matthew reveals some interesting features. Luke gives the parable as a response to some pious table talk, "Blessed is he who shall eat bread in the kingdom of God!" (Luke 14: 15). Jesus considers this remark as containing pious words that are often repeated, but to which the speaker gives little serious thought—a conventional religious slogan much like our "God bless you." The parable comes like a shock treatment introduced by the words, "*But* he said to him . . ." The cutting edge comes when the ones invited to the banquet begin to make excuses. Pious words mean nothing; they are cheap. So when the invitation comes, the true color of the slogan-slinger is revealed in his excuses. He is all for the blessedness of breaking bread in the kingdom, but when the call to respond to the banquet comes, he has his own interests that take precedence. He has a field, must examine his oxen, has just been married—all important things in themselves, and yet they stand between him and receiving the "blessedness of eating bread in the kingdom."

The other unique feature in Luke is that after such persons as the poor and the maimed are gathered by the invitation, a second scouring gathers others from highways and hedges. The Gospel according to Luke is consistently written with the gentiles in mind, and the second gathering seems to suggest that there is room for the gentiles as well as the Jews. The first gathering was from "the streets and the lanes of the city," while the second was from those in "the highways and hedges." Luke, consistent with his continual emphasis and with the heart of Jesus' message, has specifically applied the parable in such a way as to make very explicit that the invitation is to gentiles as well as to Jews. In this application he goes beyond Jesus' original statement with an allegorical flourish.

In Matthew the parable is addressed to chief priests and Pharisees who perceive that Jesus is speaking about them and who would arrest Jesus except for fear of his popularity with the multitudes. (See Matthew 21: 45–46.) When the first invitation to come to the marriage feast is extended in Matthew 22: 3, some, after the fashion of Luke's record, "made light of it and went off, one to his farm, another to his business" (Matthew 22: 5); and there is also the added category, "the rest seized his servants, treated them shamefully, and killed them" (Matthew 22: 6).

Matthew has clearly seen, in the rejection of the invitation, an analogy to the Pharisees' and chief priests' rejection of Jesus. They have seized the king's servant and killed him. But the king will send his troops and destroy the murderers, as well as extend his gracious invitation to others, "both bad and good." Matthew applies the parable to the reception Jesus received from the chief priests and Pharisees. The fact that the householder is called a king in this version makes Matthew's application of the parable to God and his servant Jesus much more pointed.

This parable has a lot in common with the previous one. An invitation to a banquet is also something freely given. It depends on the generosity of the host and not upon the qualifications of the recipient. The kingdom is like an invitation. Yet an additional note is introduced in this parable. The recipient is seen to have the responsibility of answering the invitation by coming to the feast. To ignore the invitation is to be excluded from the feast. So the gift of the kingdom is not an incentive to laziness, to human indifference, or to passiveness. Rather, it demands something from man. It demands his acceptance and action in responding to the gift. When the ones to whom the invitation is extended do not respond, the invitation is extended to those who have no prestige or merit, and they will be gathered in.

Too often we think of giving as a one-way street. A gift is something thrust upon us that we passively accept. But a gift in the teaching of Jesus is something that must be received before the action is completed. It is a two-way process. It demands something of the recipient by way of action just as much as it imparts an attitude. To make an analogy, to receive a tie for Christmas means to wear it, not to hide it on the closet shelf because of its hideous colors. As long as you store it on the closet shelf you have rejected it and giving hasn't occurred. *Giving always involves receiving, and receiving means using the gift for its intended purpose.*

It is humbling to have to receive something as a gift, for receiving implies dependence. We necessarily feel dependent upon people whose gifts support us. So when Jesus teaches that the kingdom of God is a gift, we are thrust into a position of dependence that we can never outgrow. Possessing this gift is not something that we can boast or feel self-righteous and complacent about. We might achieve an equality even with those who nurtured us, but in relation to God we must rely upon his gifts from birth to grave. The fact that the kingdom belongs to God and that we share it through his generosity makes us his debtors and cuts the ground from under all pride in our own achievements.

THE WEDDING GARMENT

We call Matthew 22:11–14 the parable of the wedding garment, but it is actually closely related to the parable of the great invitation, where "both good and bad" had been gathered from the streets by the king's invitation. In looking over his wedding guests the king discovers a guest who does not have on a wedding garment and addresses him, "Friend, how did you get in here without a wedding garment?" The requirement of wearing a wedding garment does not make sense in relation to the previous invitation to gather all from the thoroughfares. Thus, this seems to be a separate story. It does not portray the need for the disciple to be transformed by God. The garment was used as a symbol of the new life that God gave his disciples in the New Testament, and seems to have that significance here. (Compare 2 Corinthians 5: 3–4; Revelation 3: 4–5, 18: 6: 11; 7: 13.) Those who are gathered are not to judge themselves worthy or saved.

In reporting this parable Matthew seems to apply it to the church member who, though numbered in the fold, does not possess the marks of God's love and grace. Something so evident and clear as church membership can never be the test for something so hidden and mysterious as entering the kingdom of God. It is only in God's final reckoning that the hidden unclarities will be revealed to us by him. Then, and only then, shall we "understand fully," to use the words of 1 Corinthians 13: 12; and we may be in for some surprises! The final judgment, which only God can make, will illuminate the mysterious ways of the kingdom in the present and transform faith to sight.

THE PARABLE OF THE TWO SONS

The fact that we are debtors to God is brought sharply into focus by the parable of the two sons in Matthew 21: 28–31. It is told for the benefit of the Pharisees or religious people whose pious talk and status keep them from fulfilling the will of the Father. The tax collectors and harlots, however, know that their status with God depends on his gift. Jesus told the chief priests and the elders that the tax collectors and the harlots could repent and go into the kingdom before them. Notice how the story forces the Pharisees to condemn themselves out of their own mouths.

"*The kingdom of heaven may be compared to a king who gave a marriage feast for his son, and sent his servants to call those who were invited to the marriage feast; but they would not come. Again he sent other servants, saying, 'Tell those who are invited, Behold, I have made ready my dinner, my oxen and my fat calves are killed, and everything is ready; come to the marriage feast.' But they made light of it and went off, one to his farm, another to his business, while the rest seized his servants, treated them shamefully, and killed them. The king was angry, and he sent his troops and destroyed those murderers and burned their city. Then he said to his servants, 'The wedding is ready, but those invited were not worthy. Go therefore to the thoroughfares, and invite to the marriage feast as many as you find.' And those servants went out into the streets and gathered all whom they found, both bad and good; so the wedding hall was filled with guests.*" Matthew 22: 2–10

Chapter Five

THE KINGDOM HERE AND NOW

The kingdom of God in the present not only is hidden and mysterious in its working but includes in its operation men of every kind. Such inclusion within the sphere of God's working, however, is not itself a spiritual guarantee. There is a judgment upon men's response to God's gifts; and so, even though the kingdom operates widely, not all who are in the sphere of God's activity are truly responsive to his purposes. Yet all are allowed, lest harm come or gifts be denied to those who are responsive. Still, a reckoning will inevitably come when men will be judged on how they have responded to the working of the kingdom and to the use of God's gifts. The kingdom in the present gathers many. It is mixed with all kinds. Yet fruit shall be gathered, and evil judged.

The Mystery of God's Working

The kingdom of God is a gift that lays a demand upon man. This gift and demand are already operative in man's experience. Yet the gift is not discerned by everyone, and some who do recognize it are unwilling to "sell" everything in order to possess it. Jesus recognizes these problems in a series of parables that describe the operation of the kingdom of God in the present-day world. Several parables amplify the mysterious nature of God's way of working.

THE PARABLE OF THE LEAVEN

The yeast that a woman puts in a lump of dough is infinitesimally small in volume; yet the whole lump of dough is puffed up and permeated by the power of the minute amount of leaven. It bubbles in irresistible force. The parable of the leaven in Matthew 13:33 is as short as the quantity of yeast is small, but it, too, is very potent.

The potent mind was impressed by the mysterious working of the yeast. The powerful process took place in awesome fashion. The leaven dramatically, yet imperceptibly, transformed the whole lump. In this respect the parable suggests the working of the kingdom of God as a mystery. Its process cannot be discerned by the human eye. It is not the result of man's gradual and never-ending labor. It comes about without human calculation. It is pervasive, dynamic, irresistibly transforming. Hidden and unobservable though its working may be, it leaves a tremendous consequence.

In modern times we have often been inclined to misread the parable of the leaven because of our emphasis on gradual growth. This parable is often viewed through the rosy glasses of inevitable progress, but it does not suggest growth or gradual gain. It emphasizes the mystery and inevitable consequence of God's working. The parable stresses the great disproportion between the inconspicuous working of the kingdom and the tremendous consequence of this working. The kingdom in the present may be concealed from the eye, impossible to discern, hidden and small; yet it will have an inevitable and potent consequence. Though the way of God is hard to discern, it brings mighty fruit.

Life becomes confident when we accept the fact that God is mysteriously at work, even though we cannot outline his program or point out just what his plans are. When all is in God's hand, we are released—not from labor—but from anxiety about the need for success.

Not only confidence, but courage for our action, is conveyed to us in this parable. The leaven is imperceptible in relation to the lump. By sheer calculation we would have to bet on the lump every time. But the leaven, working imperceptibly, carries the day every time. Thielicke observes:

> How ridiculous it is to say: Here are a few ounces of yeast and there are two pounds of meal. According to the democratic point of view, the meal would then be the one to call the tune, because the yeast is outrated. But Jesus tells us just the opposite: It all depends on which has the real dynamic, and this is what the yeast has and not the meal. This the salt has and not the soup.[1]

The kingdom of God in the present is not manifest. It is not identified with the mass, but it carries the potency!

THE PARABLE OF THE MUSTARD SEED

Matthew has grouped the parable of the leaven with the very similar one of the mustard seed (Matthew 13: 31–32) that "is the smallest of all seeds," but when it is grown it "is the greatest of all shrubs." The emphasis is on the contrast between the seed's extreme minuteness and the shrub's great size. So the kingdom, although small, will have great consequence. While there is no stress on the mystery of the process in this parable, it is closely related to the parable of the leaven in meaning. Again the emphasis is not on the patient or gradual growth involved but on the contrast between the insignificant beginning and the tremendous ending. While it is always dangerous to press meaning out of vivid details that are not inherently part of the central emphasis, the concluding description, "becomes a tree, so that the birds of the air come and make nests in its branches," not only suggests the greatness of the resulting tree but echoes passages in Ezekiel 17: 23; 31: 6, where the figure of speech is used to suggest the harboring of the gentiles by God. Jesus, probably having this reference in mind, suggests that in its tremendous consequence the rule of God will gather nations within the fold of God's love and purpose.

It is interesting that in Luke 13: 18–19 the contrast between the size of the seed and the size of the tree is omitted. This version plays down the contrast and highlights instead the phrase "and the birds of the air made nests in its branches" as the meaning of the parable. Luke's stress on the universality of the kingdom fits well with the rest of the book of Luke, in which he presents the universal implications of the gospel; and then in the book of Acts he carries on with the story of the Spirit bringing the gospel to the whole world. Luke's application addresses a special problem of the early church, the danger of exclusiveness, and shows how Jesus' teaching bears upon it. As a result Luke bypasses the original contrast and stresses universality.

Both of these parables are described as addressed to the crowd's questions, which inevitably are, "What is God doing?" "Where is the kingdom of God?" "What is the time of the coming?" The answers constitute a promise. The reign of God is veiled; yet it possesses absolute power: "All authority in heaven and on earth!" Even within the church itself the power is veiled and is not readily apparent; yet its leaven is there. This is known to him who has the eye of faith. The confidence of Jesus probably ought to be interpreted, not as a prediction of the numerical triumph of the Christian faith, but as an indication that the kingdom of God, even when it is numerically small, has the power to transform or to leaven all of society.

These parables suggest the inconspicuous and veiled nature of the reign of God in the present, while nevertheless affirming its inevitable and tremendous consequences. The message of these parables fits closely with the basic form of the parable which conceals a mystery that can be discerned only by those with eyes to see and ears to hear. But the mystery of God's activity and the disciples' inability to comprehend it is revealed in other acts and words of Jesus as well. (See Luke 18: 31–34.)

The Kingdom Gathers Every Kind

Two other closely related parables suggest another dimension in the operation of the kingdom in the present-day world. All men, regardless of whether they are good or bad, are gathered into the kingdom of God.

THE PARABLE OF THE DRAGNET

There is a problem in interpreting the parable of the dragnet in Matthew 13: 47–50. Verses 49–50 seem to be an application of the parable that was not originally told as part of the parable. This application in verses 49–50 lays its stress on the separation of the good and the bad by emphasizing the last judgment and the punishment of evil. This stress seems to have been a special interest of part of the early church, and it occurs at several points in this Gospel. (See Matthew 13: 40–42.)

The parable of the dragnet is actually complete in verses 47 and 48. The kingdom of God, pictured there, is like a net "which was thrown into the sea and gathered fish of every kind." The kingdom gathers all kinds of people. As a gift it reaches out recklessly for all. It does not bring in a single type of person, nor does it gather only the good people, but many kinds. And yet when the process is complete a separation is made between the good and the bad. The implication is that while the kingdom gathers many kinds of people in the present, accounting will nevertheless be made. To be caught in the sweep and the swirl of the kingdom is not a blanket guarantee of value or worth. If we accept Matthew's placement of the parable as addressd to the disciples, inevitably the application of the parable is that in their missionary proclamation all kinds of followers will be gathered. It is not up to the disciples to decide who is acceptable. They are to preach the word, and the kingdom will gather all kinds—tax collectors, zealots, fishermen. Separation is left to take place at the end of time.

The concluding verses, unfortunately, tend to shift the whole application of the parable, making it sound as though it were solely a picture of the last judgment, with emphasis upon the terror of what will happen to the unrighteous. But the parable stresses that the kingdom gathers every kind in its present operation. Even among God's people there will be some included who do not belong. Yet we are not to worry over that, for the separation will be made at the end. Rather than stressing the horrors of judgment, the parable explains the presence of unsuitable types gathered among God's people, on the grounds that separation comes only when the process is complete. As in the leaven, the process now at work has an inevitable conclusion in judgment—but this is God's work, not ours.

THE PARABLE OF THE WHEAT AND THE TARES

The parable of the wheat and the tares in Matthew 13: 24–30 develops a similar idea. The interpretation of this parable is difficult because it is one of the two parables for which explanations are offered in the text of the Gospel. Such a recording of an explanation of a parable strikes an unusual note. It was not Jesus' method to dish out answers in such a way that no insight was demanded of the hearer. In fact, one of the important distinguishing marks of parables is that they demand something of the hearer and drive home their meaning because the hearer must grasp for this meaning. Hence, an explanation is not only atypical, but seems to contradict Jesus' whole purpose. The second startling thing about the explanation is that what is called a parable is really interpreted as if it were an allegory. The interpretation is allegorical rather than parabolic.

Let us see what meaning the story might have. In the parable the good grain and the weeds come up side by side. Upon the expressed readiness of the servants to uproot the weeds the householder replies, "No; lest in gathering the weeds you root up the wheat along with them. Let both grow together until harvest." (Matthew 13: 29–30). The good and evil are so closely intertwined in the world that it is impossible to destory or discard the one without risking permanent damage to the other. It is like the police refusing to shoot at fleeing robbers on a crowded street, lest the innocent be hurt. So it is suggested that the two are to be allowed to grow together, lest the good be destroyed. God allows the evil to exist for the sake of the good so that the good might reach maturity. (Compare with Genesis 18: 22–33.)

Now let us look at the allegorical explanation of the parable of the wheat and the tares that is given in Matthew 13: 36–43. In this interpretation, the emphasis falls not on the inevitable intermingling of good and evil in this world, with stress on the fact that evil is allowed to survive so that the good might be given a chance to grow, but rather on the last judgment and the contrast between the final fate of evildoers and the reward of the righteous. Here, what was only the concluding part of the parable is made the basis for the major part of the interpretation. The allegorical interpretation of this parable implies that the story is not a description of life at all, but only veiled references to the Son of man, the devil, and the last judgment. None of these can stand for God and his purposes. Allegorizing takes the vividness of a real life situation from the parable and makes it only an artificial story that has nothing to do with its seeming subject. "'He who sows the good seed is the Son of man; the field is the world, and the good seed means the sons of the kingdom; the weeds are the sons of the evil one, and the enemy who sowed them is the devil; the harvest is the close of the age, and the reapers are angels'" (Matthew 13: 37–39).

Consequences of Encounter
with the Kingdom of God

As we encounter the kingdom's action in the present, the application seems direct. The final judgment belongs to God—and at the end of things. It cannot be calculated in the present, least of all by us. This has several consequences:

1. Judge not. The rule of God is too concealed to discern its working. For us to pick out its reality is too presumptuous. Such action implies that God is subject to our judgment and liable to our discrimination. It makes us lords and belittles him, all at the same time.

2. We must not take for granted our own standing in the kingdom of God. All kinds are gathered by the invitation to the banquet. Wheat and tares grow together in the same field; all kinds of fish are gathered together in the dragnet. To be in the dragnet is no guarantee of being pronounced good; to be in the field of God's planting does not guarantee that we are wheat rather than weed.

3. Since God offers his kingdom to all people, it is not our role to limit its appeal by any human criteria.

4. It is not only impossible for man to make any ultimate distinction between persons, but good and evil are confused in each of us. The wheat and the tares are in every life. Occasionally a hero has decided to root out all of the tares in himself. Without raising the question of the possibility of such a procedure, the questions remain: Which are the tares? By what means does God work to produce a harvest? You went to church out of curiosity for the first time, and God used your curiosity to win you to himself. Curiosity isn't a satisfactory reason for being in church. Are you not going to do anything out of curiosity from now on? Was the curiosity wheat or tare?

A young fellow entered the ministry because he loved to stand before the multitudes and preach. It satisfied his ego.

This is not a good reason for entering the ministry. Should he henceforth do nothing that he enjoys or that gives satisfaction to himself? Through some such men God has worked mighty acts. Who judges what kind of fish the dragnet of the ministry has gathered? Do we root out those who find satisfaction in preaching? Who can separate the weeds and the wheat when they look so much alike?

"A man had a fig tree planted in his vineyard; and he came seeking fruit on it and found none. And he said to the vine-dresser, 'Lo, these three years I have come seeking fruit on this fig tree, and I find none. Cut it down; why should it use up the ground?' And he answered him, 'Let it alone, sir, this year also, till I dig about it and put on manure. And if it bears fruit next year, well and good; but if not, you can cut it down.'"

Luke 13: 6–9

Chapter Six

PARABLES OF CRISIS

While the fact that the kingdom of God is a gift makes clear that it is the good news of salvation, the kingdom of God also comes with a cry of warning and as an announcement of judgment. The parables of crises reveal a people who cannot discern the signs of the times and who are rushing to destruction. As ambiguous as things may be, we must discern the indicators and glimpse the signals of God's action in the present, lest we be destroyed. The kingdom is not manifestly here; but its outposts and scouts are already at work, and these must be recognized.

While the kingdom operates mysteriously in the present and gathers people of every kind in its liberality, the parables of crises clarify both of these functions. The manifest appearance of the kingdom is still to come. At that time, the works of men will be revealed to themselves and to others. These parables really view life from the viewpoint of God's perfected action. No longer, in the light of the end, is the operation of the kingdom mysterious; no longer does it gather the good and the bad!

Preparedness for the Unexpected

Several parables inform us of one aspect of crisis in our lives. Since the kingdom of God comes at a time of his choosing rather than ours, and often in a mysterious manner, we must always be prepared for the unexpected.

THE PARABLE OF THE TEN MAIDENS

One of the parables concerning preparedness is the parable of the ten maidens. (See Matthew 25: 1–13.) In reading it one sees how easy it is to get distracted by the story if one tries to make a moral example of its content. The wise maidens appear selfish in refusing to lend oil to the foolish. But the story is told neither to suggest that this type of behavior is condoned nor to condemn it. This is part of a complete story with a realistic tone.

The highlight of this parable is the readiness of the wise maidens and the folly of the unprepared. Even as the bridegroom comes at the unexpected hour, and those who are not prepared miss the marriage feast; so also the kingdom of God (his rule) comes unexpectedly, and there will be found at its feast only those who are ready for it. The kingdom demands preparedness. "Watch therefore." The kingdom is about to break in. If we are not prepared for it, we will find ourselves shut out. The coming kingdom brings a judgment upon life.

It is interesting that watching is not interpreted as perpetual waiting in the parable. Both the wise and the foolish slumber, and there is no criticism implied. The wise, however, are ready for the coming of the bridegroom, regardless of circumstances. The foolish are not. It is not sleep and wakefulness that are contrasted, but unreadiness and preparedness for any eventuality.

The difference between the ten maidens would never have been apparent if the bridegroom had arrived as expected. The wise maidens were prepared, not for the expected, but for the unexpected. It was this readiness that made them wise in contrast to the foolish. The parable does not demand perpetual religiosity nor does it condemn sleep, but it commends preparedness for any situation of life.

The coming of this rule occurs often in the least expected and most unusual circumstances of life, for it is in the unexpected situation that our lives are tested. When things are normal our habits and routines carry on; but in the unusual events there are no habits to fall back upon, and we reveal the inner character of which we are made. God's coming to us is always unexpected; we cannot calculate his ways, and therefore it always brings a crisis in our lives and a testing of what we are. It is this testing, rather than "Watch," that is the subject of the biblical parable.

The preparedness for the unexpected can carry a strong moral emphasis. Morality is not a matter of doing right purely from conventional habit; it is also doing right when there is no precedence or set of community patterns. For example, it is morally wrong when people who would normally never think of stealing, freely take what is not their own if it is found in an unusual place. A friend had a tent fall from the roof of his car while he was traveling. Before he found a place to turn around and come back the tent was gone. From the standpoint of good morals, the person who took it would probably never think of stealing a tent if it were found in the usual place—pitched in a campsite, or on the shelf of a store.

This moral aspect of the crisis of the kingdom is portrayed vividly in the parable of the servant placed in authority. When he assumes the master is not coming, the servant acts irresponsibly as a steward, misusing both things and people. (See Luke 12: 42–48 and Matthew 24: 45–51.)

Responsibility for Entrusted Gifts

A series of three parables in Matthew and Luke has a similar message of preparedness occasioned by the imminent coming of the kingdom.

Included in the series are the parables of the burglar (Luke 12: 39–40 and Matthew 24: 43–44), the waiting servants (Luke 12: 35–38), and the servant placed in authority (Luke 12: 42–48 and Matthew 24: 45–51).

The Parable of the Burglar

The parable of the burglar in Luke 12: 39–40 and Matthew 24: 43–44 concerns a man whose house was broken into. If he had known when the burglar was coming he would have been ready. So the hour of God's breaking into life is at hand. When addressed to the disciples, as here, the parable suggests that the time of stress is at hand and the disciples must be prepared for it. Later this idea was reapplied to persistent readiness for the second coming. This is made evident by what precedes the parable of the burglar in Matthew 24: 42.

The Waiting Servants

In the parable of the waiting servants in Luke 12: 35–38, the servants are expectant and poised for the coming of the master. The disciple must just as eagerly be ready to grasp the gift of the kingdom. (Compare the setting given in Luke 12: 32.) Blessed are those who are thus ready.

The Parable of the Servant Placed in Authority

The final parable in this series of three is that of the servant placed in authority. (See Luke 12: 42–48 and Matthew 24: 45–51.) As the servant does not know the hour of his master's coming, he may be tempted to assume that his master is delayed. When this occurs, he may be tempted to begin "to beat the menservants and maidservants, and to eat and drink and get drunk," instead of faithfully and wisely carrying out his given responsibilities as steward. Responsibility may give way to self-exaltation and self-indulgence. In Matthew the text says that the steward will be put with hypocrites as a result. Hypocrites are play actors—pretending to be stewards—when they are really self-centered. The true steward faithfully fulfills his responsibility because the coming, the hour of reckoning, is always at an unexpected time.

Perhaps the greatest danger in the fact that the kingdom

is hidden and that its ways are hard to discern is the assumption that it is delayed or not coming at all. The future does not seem to belong to God because his way in the present is hard to discern. But when the future does not belong to God the present loses its significance, and God's signs are quickly forgotten or overlooked. When the servant gives up the expectation of the master's coming, he may lose respect and interest in the present and quickly align himself with the forces of destruction. (See Luke 12: 45–46.) It is a great fact that all of life must be confronted with the coming rule of God if the present is to have crucial relevance. Jesus' teaching that the coming kingdom is already breaking in provides the consciousness that life now is confronted by the ultimate will and judgment of God.

An Urgent Reorientation of Life

Along with the demand for preparedness, the kingdom sounds a tone of *urgency*. Not only must one be prepared, but the full rule of God is imminent. It is just around the corner; it is on the verge of breaking into the world in fullness. This sense of the closeness and immediacy of God gives an urgency to the message. One must already live by its demands. There is no time to squander. Action now determines one's relation to this overwhelming reality.

THE PARABLE OF THE DEFENDANT

It is this kind of setting that the parable of the defendant implies as it is found in Luke 12: 57–59. Settle with your accuser on the way to the magistrate. If you wait, you will be handed over to the judge. The judge is a figure of ultimate judgment, and there is no escaping him.

We find that definite action must be taken as we read in Luke 12: 59: "I tell you, you will never get out till you have paid the very last copper."

61

THE PARABLE OF THE BARREN FIG TREE

The parable of the barren fig tree in Luke 13: 6–9 carries the tone of urgency to a climax. A man has been looking for fruit from his fruit tree; yet the tree refuses to bear. Since it does not fulfill its function the owner determines to cut it down. The vinedresser pleads for the tree and vows to nourish it if it is given just one more chance; saying that, if after the tree is cultivated and fertilized it still fails to bear fruit, the owner can cut it down. This will provide one more chance before the decisive step is taken.

The one chance offered is a call to repentance. This parable is a vivid illustration of a remark made in the previous incident as it is recorded in Luke 13: 5, "Unless you repent you will all likewise perish." The sense of crisis leads to the demand for self-reorientation. The word *repent* comes from the word *return* or *turn around*. What is called for in repentance is to live life in a new direction—organized around a different point of focus.

The coming of the reign of God in its fullness carries a twofold demand: (1) urgency (a demand for repentance) and (2) preparation (responsibility for entrusted gifts). The coming kingdom is morally relevant to the present moment. It is a spur to action that gives heightened significance to the here and now. Repentance and moral responsibility are intimately connected with the idea that the kingdom is coming in its totality. Its coming makes the action of the present crucial. Failure to bear fruit responsibly means the necessity of a judgment of rejection. There is a crisis; God rules over all of us, and all of us are responsible to him.

The parables of the coming kingdom do not present the rule of God as an event that is irrelevant to the present. Too often the coming of the kingdom has been as unrelated to the present moment as a fortune teller's prediction is irrelevant to current events. The crystal ball paints the future as some dim and far-off event that comes as a surprise out of the blue. The coming of the kingdom of God is not a dim event in the future. Its signs and advanced outposts can already be noted, and the way one relates himself to these signs and advanced activities establishes his final status in the kingdom. God is bringing the kingdom in its power. Yet its power is already at work, though it cannot be seen or measured with the eyes of the world, but only with the eyes of faith. The way we live in relation to this inconspicuous power inevitably sets our relation to the final power.

That which faith hopes for, the Christian already knows and lives by, just as the steward knows his master and the way he wants his accounts handled even while waiting for his coming. It is only when the steward loses the awareness of the master's control and final accounting, that he begins to mishandle the wealth entrusted to him and acts dishonorably toward others and himself.

The Consequences of One's Action

Our actions do make a difference. Ultimately they meet with their consequences.

THE STORY (OR VISION) OF THE LAST JUDGMENT

Perhaps this is revealed most decisively in the story of the last judgment (see Matthew 25: 31–46), which is not so much a parable as a story or vision of the end. Final judgment pictures the ultimate consequence of human behavior. The Son of man (as King in this story) has come to inaugurate the kingdom that comes from the Father. Some men are invited to participate. They did the works of the King by providing food, drink, welcome, clothing, comfort, and consolation. Having done this to the King's subjects was as having done it to him. Yet it is important to observe that those who receive the commendation do not understand why they are thus commended. While there is a final judgment with the coming kingdom, this judgment is not presented as the motive for man's actions. Men have acted responsibly, but they did not know that they acted for the King.

While the parables of the leaven and the dragnet dealt with the present order of the kingdom, they did not isolate it from the future; though they portrayed its inevitable consequences. In the story of the last judgment we have a parable presenting the future kingdom; yet the future cannot be dealt with without portraying how it relates to the present. The King is here now, but was hidden before as the future Judge. (See Matthew 25: 37.) The judgment will inevitably involve one's present attitude to the forgotten people of society. Parables of the coming of the kingdom in its fullness and of the present activity of the kingdom inevitably merge together. Parables of the coming of the kingdom in its wholeness inevitably deal with the present moment; parables concerning the present inevitably deal with the coming of the kingdom in its fullness.

The vision reveals a profound sense of the double interpretation of the Son of man figure. In Jewish apocalyptic writings, the Son of man is an exalted figure who comes on the clouds in glory to judge and to rule. Combined with this is the gospel picture of the King's identification with all of his subjects. He is sympathetic with all human sufferers—the hungry, the estranged, the naked, the imprisoned: "As you did it to one of the least of these my brethren, you did it to me." The King is one with the least and the last—friend of tax collectors and sinners.

The gifts of God are the motive for action in Jesus' parables, and not the threat of such things as judgment, hell, and fire. Yet at the same time the coming kingdom does bring a judgment upon men's actions. It is relevant to present moral actions, and men have already determined their relation to the kingdom by the way they have acted in history.

The coming of the kingdom in fullness heightens the need for repentance and the moral responsibility of man. Wherever there has been a religion that took moral decision in historic life seriously there has been a concept of final judgment. While judgment is not the last word in Christianity, since God's gifts are the overarching reality; yet within the framework of the gift of the coming kingdom there is the concept of judgment. Judgment is not the final word, but it is a real word; and the King of this kingdom has as one of his roles that of judge.

The Interdependence of Present and Future

But what is the relation of the coming of the kingdom in its fullness to the partial operation of it in the present? They are interdependent. If either of these two facets is stressed without reference to the other, the result is disastrous. If the kingdom is proclaimed only as a present reality, we lose all perspective of God as Judge of the present. We accept all as it now exists as being divinely willed; for example, we call tares wheat, and evil good. We glorify the present order of things. We carry on our religion through self-righteous activity, and endeavor to keep aloof from contamination.

When we stress the kingdom as present only, we forget that God's way is in part veiled from our eyes and that good and evil exist side by side. The coming of the kingdom in its fullness stands as a judgment upon the present in relation to the final order of things. The kingdom in its fullness reminds us that in the present the reign of God is veiled, and his way is different from the way of the world. When we understand this fact, we are moved to probe for the tares in order to discern the wheat.

And yet if we only stress the kingdom coming in its fullness, we lose the relevance of the reign of God to life here and now. Life in the here and now becomes divorced from

God's purpose and will. When we realize that the kingdom of God is already present, it reminds us that the God whose final works are still to come is already at work. The same God whose final purpose is known, rules over the ambiguous activity of the present.

Where the present signs of the kingdom are neglected, the present loses meaning and religion dreams of the future. Salvation is thought of as a future state and the world is abandoned to non-Christian leadership, since it lies outside the sphere of salvation. We rebel against groups that make religion a matter of waiting for the second coming or "pie in the sky" and which abandon the world and society as evil and beyond God's care, but who find no means of recognizing their own immoral behavior in the present. To stress the kingdom as exclusively present or future is to lose its dynamic relevance to life. It ceases to be yeast in the lump.

The relationship between the kingdom in the present and the future is expressed in the fact that signs of the fulfilled kingdom are already manifest and indicate its actuality and nearness. The healings of Jesus are interpreted as signs of the kingdom as it works its power in the present. The kingdom is already evident wherever evil and sin are being overcome. This inevitably means a crisis, because the onslaught against evil is underway.

The Parables of the Budding Fig Tree
and the Householder

There are additional parables of crisis that the coming of the kindom inaugurates. The parable of the budding fig tree (see Mark 13: 28) and the story of the householder (see Luke 13: 25–30) both present aspects of the urgency of the kingdom. The budding fig tree suggests that just as the signs of summer are already present, so also signs of the kingdom suggest its imminent reality. The parable of the householder indicates that when the kingdom has come in its fullness it is too late to establish a relationship with it. The relation is determined by the way in which we respond to its present and veiled working. In like manner, the way in which we respond now to the Inaugurator of the kingdom determines our destiny when the kingdom arrives in its fullness.

In chapter ten of the Gospel according to Luke, the reception accorded the seventy who were commissioned and sent forth was an indication of the way the Sender is received. "He who hears you hears me." (Luke 10: 16). Our relation to the kingdom which is to come in its fullness is closely related to our relation to the kingdom that is in our midst, whose working is hidden; whose gate is narrow and hard to discern; whose operation in the present includes both the good and the bad—the weeds and the wheat—the separation of which will not be made until the kingdom has come in its fullness.

"Again, the kingdom of heaven is like a merchant in search of fine pearls, who, on finding one pearl of great value, went and sold all that he had and bought it." Matthew 13:45–46

Chapter Seven

ENTERING
THE KINGDOM

One of the criticisms of the teaching of Jesus is that if the kingdom of God is a gift, all that man has to do is to gather its benefits just as a teller at a bank window gathers money. Jesus' graciousness toward tax collectors and sinners never meant a lessening of the absolute commitment that was demanded of a disciple. There rings constantly in the teaching of Jesus the need for obedience that must be given an absolute God no matter how gracious he may be. The more personal is God, the more unconditional is the surrender of the total person demanded by the gospel. "No one who puts his hand to the plow and looks back is fit for the kingdom of God" (Luke 9: 62).

This is of immense importance in considering what is involved in entering the kingdom of God. Our every study and contemplation of the graciousness of God tends to entice us into the misconception that there are few if any requirements for entrance into the kingdom.

There is no other religion or religious teaching that lays as exacting a claim upon our lives as does that of Jesus. Love of the sinner is not an overlooking of moral responsibility. "Follow me," a command that occurs frequently in the Gospels, puts a complete claim on our lives. An absolute God demands an absolute response—one hundred percent of our loyalty and being. We must live by the veiled but wonderful power of the kingdom!

Singleness of Purpose

The parable of the invitation to the banquet (wedding feast), discussed in chapter four, provides a transition to this subject because an invitation always demands a response. There are other parables in addition to this one that lay stress on human responsibility, where singleness of purpose is prominent. Two of these are the parable of the hidden treasure and the parable of the pearl of great price. Both of these are so short that it is virtually impossible to get diverted to side issues or to be involved in distracting excursions away from the heart of the parable.

THE PARABLE OF THE HIDDEN TREASURE

In the parable of the hidden treasure (see Matthew 13: 44), a man found a treasure in the field. Then he went and sold all that he had in order to buy the field. Once he found the treasure, it was worth all that he had in order to obtain it—and he gave that all. Furthermore, such surrender was no sacrifice; rather, it was the occasion for joy. He had found the one thing worth having. This is the whole of the parable.

To ask whether the man might have been defrauding the owner is to ask a question that misses the mark. There is no concern with the owner, or whether an adequate fee was paid. The single point of likeness is that as the man who found the treasure gave his all to possess it with joy, so the kingdom of God when found is worth all that one has. To worry about any other aspect of the parable is to divert from the issue.

THE PARABLE OF THE PEARL OF GREAT PRICE

The parable of the pearl of great price (see Matthew 13: 45–46), while using a different story, makes a similar point—the pearl of great value is worth all that one has. This story, however, omits two minor details that are contained in the parable of the hidden treasure. No mention is made of the joy that comes in selling all that one has in order to possess the costly pearl, and no indication is given as to whether the man who found the treasure was diligently seeking or came upon it accidentally. The merchant, on the other hand, is portrayed as being in search of fine pearls. Quite clearly the issue is not whether one seeks diligently or not. These are not parables on "keep trying." Whether we stumble on the treasure or whether we search for it is unimportant. These variations make the central point of the parables more clear, and so these parables are grouped together in the Scriptures.

While the kingdom is God's and is dependent upon his effort and generosity, many of the parables stress our responsibility to put forth all that we have in order to possess that gift. The gift brings a demand. The detail of how we discover the gift is not central, nor is it always the same; but we must respond by surrendering all interests in order to claim the one thing of great value. Such a surrender is to lose nothing, but to gain all.

Readiness to Pay the Cost

The fact that discipleship involves a cost is vividly expressed in two companion parables, the costly tower and the rash king.

THE COSTLY TOWER

Jesus tells a parable asking who begins to build a tower without first sitting down and counting the cost. (See Luke 14: 28–30.) Jesus said that if we do not first carefully count the cost and consider whether we will be able to complete the project, we will find that when we have laid the foundation and are unable to finish, all who see it will mock us.

THE RASH KING

Likewise, in the parable of the rash king in Luke 14:31–32, a king going into battle will first sit down and calculate whether his forces are adequate to meet the enemy; if not, he will seek terms of peace before engaging in battle.

Before becoming a disciple of Jesus, we must consider whether we are willing to meet the demand that is involved. To begin as a disciple without being ready to pay the cost can only mean ridicule, even as a man is mocked who begins to build without being able to finish. It would be better if we had never made a profession in the first place.

In *Pilgrim's Progress,* John Bunyan tells of two who began their journey to the eternal city—one was Christian and the other Pliable. When Pliable came to the first obstacle, the Slough of Despond, he turned back and went home convinced that there was a discrepancy between the eternal city with its promises and his actual experience of difficulty. Sometime later Christian heard word of Pliable through a new pilgrim, Faithful, who had joined him. Christian asked what had happened to Pliable after his return to the City of Destruction.

Christian: And what said the neighbours to him?

Faithful: He hath since his going back been had greatly in derision, and that among all sorts of people; some do mock and despise him; and scarce will any set him on work. He is now seven times worse than if he had never gone out of the city.

Christian: But why should they be so set against him, since they also despise the way that he forsook?

Faithful: Oh, they say, hang him, he is a turn-coat, he was not true to his profession. I think God has stirred up even his enemies to hiss at him and make him a proverb, because he hath forsaken the way.

Christian: Had you no talk with him before you came out?

Faithful: I met him once in the streets, but he leered away on the other side, as one ashamed of what he had done; so I spake not to him.[1]

Likewise, in the parable of the costly tower while the mockery is not stressed, the essential wisdom of knowing whether we can carry through what we begin is portrayed. If we cannot carry through, we must make other arrangements rather than to begin what we cannot accomplish.

Jesus concludes these two parables with the statement, "So therefore, whoever of you does not renounce all that he has cannot be my disciple" (Luke 14: 33). Before entering on a life of discipleship we must be aware of the obligations involved. If we cannot meet them, we had better not begin— lest God foreclose on us.

These two parables are reported to have been delivered to the multitudes when they were following Jesus in great numbers. Undoubtedly their purpose and effect at a time of apparent success and popularity was to remind the followers that this was serious business. There was a sacrifice involved. The gospel was not a popularity movement sweeping the religious drifters and the curious in its train. The cost was very likely a shock to many in the multitude, and failure to meet the cost would subject them to mockery and shame.

The cost is set forth in the severest terms. "If any one comes to me and does not hate his own father and mother and wife and children and brothers and sisters, yes, and even his own life, he cannot be my disciple. Whoever does not bear his own cross and come after me, cannot be my disciple" (Luke 14: 26–27). For one who talked about loving his enemies such words seem extremely severe. Yet they are as crucial and as much a part of the gospel as Jesus' words about loving one's enemies. Unfortunately, we have emphasized the "love of enemy" and missed the "hate family and his own life." Neither can be kept in focus without the other.

The danger implied in Luke 14: 26–27 is the temptation to put ourself or our own group in place of God. Family love can be the highest expression of religious experience; but it can also become an end in itself, doting on its own emotions.

73

(Compare Luke 14: 18–21.) The family must be given up for the sake of God, even as the pearl merchant gave up all that he had in order to possess the pearl of great value. But when this is done, it always turns out that God gives back the family, transformed by his Spirit and love. To surrender to God is to lose nothing at all, but to gain all.

Perhaps our basic law of responsibility is not revealed in any parable of Jesus so much as in a statement following a discussion upon the parable of the servant placed in authority. The statement is, "Every one to whom much is given, of him will much be required; and of him to whom men commit much they will demand the more" (Luke 12: 48). The discussion distinguishes between faithful and unfaithful stewards: (1) The faithful and wise steward is blessed. (2) The steward who not only concludes that the master is delayed but uses this as an opportunity to grasp power, and lives shamefully, will be punished and cast out among the unfaithful. (3) The servant who knows the master's will but did not make ready to act according to that will, receives a severe beating. (4) The servant who did what was wrong but did not know, will receive a light beating. Here we see a wide divergence of consequences because of differing knowledge and action.

THE PARABLE OF THE DISHONEST STEWARD

The parable of the dishonest steward in Luke 16: 1–8 is very fascinating because the central figure of the parable is a scoundrel. Here we see clearly that the parable is a story complete in itself which must not be taken as a moral example for life. The dishonest steward upon hearing that he was losing his job falsified the accounts by reducing the amounts owned by each of his master's debtors—in order to win their favor. In a tight situation he used the means that were his to secure his future. Jesus commends the "sons of this world" for being wiser than "the sons of light."

If only the sons of light were as eager and clever in using their capacities in seeking the light they would be worthy sons of the kingdom of God. Cleverness must be used just as diligently in the service of God as in the bettering of our own lot. As T. W. Manson states, there is a difference between commending the dishonest steward for his cleverness and commending the clever steward for his dishonesty.[2]

The Willingness to Venture

The parable of the talents (see Matthew 25: 14–30 and Luke 19: 11–27) is one of the most difficult to interpret in its original setting because of the varied emphasis it has received in the New Testament and subsequently. Like the parable of the dishonest steward, while it has money as its subject it is not about the use of money, but about God's relation to man and man's responsibilities. It must not be treated as a story on the correct use of money anymore than the parable of the seed growing of itself is meant to be advice on farming or the parable of the dishonest steward is meant to reveal the correct way for us to win friends and influence people.

There are some radical differences between Matthew and Luke in the telling of this parable. Since Matthew's form of the parable is the familiar one, let us begin by attempting to interpret it. A departing master has entrusted his property to his servants, dividing it according to their ability. The significant issue in the parable is that the master is wroth with the one servant who buried the talent, but not with the others. (Remember that the master is not God, but that this is a realistic, human story, which reveals at some point of emphasis the divine-human relationship.) Both of the first two servants pleased the master with their use of the talents and received his blessing, which is phrased "enter into the joy of your master." The consequences are the same for both in spite of the fact that they dealt in unequal amounts. The master in the story acts in accordance with the principle that to whom much is given, of him will much be required.

The crucial and difficult issue in the story is to follow the reasoning of the third servant. By the rule of "end stress" the emphasis of the parable falls on this servant and his action rather than on the other two. He says, "Master, I knew you to be a hard man, reaping where you did not sow, and gathering where you did not winnow" (Matthew 25:24). The master demands what is not his own. He gathers what he did not sow. He is a hard man. Because the master is so hard, the servant was afraid when he possessed the master's talent. If the master is so harsh that he demands what is not his, how much more dangerous it would be if one should lose what the master had given! Out of fear the servant went and hid his money lest he lose it and have to face the master's wrath. When the master returns the servant comes triumphantly and says in effect, "Whew! Here you have what is yours." The pressure is off. The exacting taskmaster did not lose his talent in the fearful servant's hands. The fearful servant is like a housewife who has been loaned an expensive and irreplaceable vase to keep for a friend. She locks it in a cabinet so that the children will not get at it or break it. The woman sighs in relief when she is able to return the vase undamaged.

But it is precisely this attitude that brings the master's stern rebuke. The servant's own words condemn him. Since he knew the master to be a harsh man, demanding much more than was his, he should have made sure that he would return much more than had been entrusted to him. It was the very harshness of the master that had made him cautious to keep intact the master's possessions, but which should have led him to see that he must return more; for the master wanted back more than he gave. For failing to give back more, the talent is taken from him. God's gifts are not to be merely preserved; they must bear additional fruit. Here we see the aptness of the financial basis of the parable. When you lend out money you expect interest. So God expects a demonstrable return from the use of his gifts.

The man with the one talent protected what was given him but was unwilling to venture it. This is like honoring religion—believing that it is important in society, not wanting a godless world, perhaps getting baptized and married in the church—but refusing to live by its power. This is also like being unwilling to invest one's life and risk all for the sake of God. The one-talent man has protected himself from risk. He doesn't renounce his trust, but stores it—unwilling to live by it. At the climax the talent is retracted from the cautious middle-of-the-roader, for he condemned himself in his own words when he tried to serve a demanding master by fearing to venture. God cannot be served by complacency or caution.

"For to every one who has will more be given, and he will have abundance; but from him who has not, even what he has will be taken away" (Matthew 25: 29). This seems to prejudge the issue in terms of the quantity of the original gift. It was originally an independent saying that was included here in the Gospel of Matthew because it seemed related to the action of the preceding verses. While setting forth the general teaching of Jesus (compare Matthew 13: 12), it does not express the meaning of the parable that has been told. "And cast the worthless servant into the outer darkness; there men will weep and gnash their teeth" (Matthew 25: 30) is a combination of favorite expressions of Matthew (8: 12; 13: 42, 50; 22: 13; 24: 51 and 25: 30). Other than in the Gospel of Matthew, "Cast . . . into the outer darkness" occurs in no other book in the New Testament, while "weep and gnash . . . teeth" is found only in Luke 13: 28.

In the Gospel according to Luke the parable of the talents (Luke 19: 11–27) shows some major variations. The immediate reason for telling the parable is "because they supposed that the kingdom of God was to appear immediately." The context implies that the parable was told to ex-

77

plain the delay in the coming of the kingdom while in Matthew it was told to advise watchfulness for the return of the master who will expect fruit from his investment. Watching is a call for action. The preceding parable of the ten maidens in Matthew has the same point, and the following parable deals with the last judgment. Thus, the application of the parable of the talents in Luke differs from that suggested in Matthew.

The nobleman (not master in Luke) is absent, for he has gone to inherit a kingdom. Before leaving, the nobleman gives ten servants ten pounds. In Luke's version all receive the same amount. This dissimilarity suggests that the amount was not the focal point of the parable. At the time of the reckoning the first servant has increased his pound by ten pounds, and the second by five pounds; but the third returns his single pound and gives the same reason that was recorded in Matthew. Luke's account adds the clarifying comment that the nobleman will condemn the servant out of his own mouth. The nobleman asks the servant why he did not invest the money so that it could be collected with interest—since the servant was aware of his severity. While the details differ, the crux is the same as in Matthew's account. The gift should have been used to please the master's desires.

In the Lukan form of the parable the saying "I tell you, that to every one who has will more be given; but from him who has not, even what he has will be taken away" (Luke 19: 26) makes much more sense in relation to the parable because it is not a judgment that reflects on the varying amounts which the nobleman has given. They were all given an equal amount. Rather, it reflects on the servant's fear that kept him from meeting the harsh demands of the nobleman. He had little because in his fear of the nobleman's severity he did not feel free to risk what was his master's. The result was that he returned the small amount.

Originally there probably were only three servants in the

parable. The additional seven in Luke most likely accumulated in retelling the parable because of confusion with the ten pounds. Similarly, in the original story each servant was most likely given the same amount as recorded in Luke. The varying amounts in Matthew might reflect the fact that the story was associated with the other saying, "For to every one who has will more be given, and he will have abundance; but from him who has not, even what he has will be taken away" (Matthew 25: 29).

To whom was this parable originally addressed? What was the situation in which Jesus told it? Matthew applies it to the disciples of the early church. Taken by itself it seems to teach the need for responsibility and willingness to venture for the sake of God that is demanded of us. Matthew 25: 29 adds a generalized teaching related to this responsibility. In the context of the other sayings of chapters 24 and 25, this verse speaks to the crisis of God's final judgment. (Compare Matthew 25: 30.)

All of these applications of this parable relate to concerns and needs of disciples in the early church. Matthew especially applies the sayings of Jesus to the disciples and to the needs of followers of Christ—church members. Jesus' original application has probably not been preserved. This parable could have been told against the Pharisees, for it carries a strong criticism. Remember that by end stress the point of the parable falls on the disciple who buried his talent, not on those who used it rightly, which would have to be the case if it were told originally as an example for the disciples to follow.

What is the criticism of the Pharisee? He puts a hedge around his faith to keep it from being contaminated. Instead of investing it or putting it to work in the world, he keeps it pure by isolating it from bad influences. The Pharisees did not share their faith with tax collectors and sinners for fear that such contact would contaminate themselves and their faith. A parallel would be the missionary who goes to India

79

to convert the Hindus—there is always the chance that the Hindus will convert him. The Pharisees thought God wanted them to be separate, pure and uncontaminated by contact with unclean people. They were unwilling to add to or risk the precious gift, but hedged it about. There may well be sarcasm in the fact that the parable uses as its metaphor the investing of money. The implied sarcasm of Jesus might sound something like: "You are willing to do business with foreigners and unclean people, but you are unwilling to trade the faith with them, assuming that it is for yourselves alone. You store it like money put in a sock." This hits home when one thinks of how we do business with all people, but seldom share our faith. Internationally, American business is exported throughout the world, but many are hesitant to seek to evangelize non-Christian people.

Confidence in the Gospel

Another important responsibility in discipleship is the sharing of the good news of God.

THE PARABLE OF THE SOWER

The sharing of this good news is most clearly set forth in the parable of the sower in Matthew 13: 1–23; Mark 4: 1–20; and Luke 8: 4–15. The interpretation in Luke 8: 11–15 makes our understanding of this parable difficult for several reasons: (1) The interpretation treats the story as an allegory and not a parable. Each object is treated as a veiled reference for something else. Yet the story has all the characteristics of a true-to-life experience. (2) Such interpretations, which are given in this fashion only twice in the Gospels, seem to deny the very purpose for which the parables are told. They give the answer, and so do not cause the hearer to grasp for the meaning. (3) The explanation in Mark follows the statement which implies that parables were used to keep people from understanding. The disciples need to be given a secret key for understanding this parable. The interpretation makes Jesus appear to give a secret wisdom to insiders.

If we look back at the parable of the sower as a parable, and forget for a moment the interpretation given, certain features become evident: (1) The emphasis in the parable is on the sower. As he sowed, quantities of seed fell in places where growth to harvest was impossible. (2) There is a three-fold description of why the seed failed to grow. This three-fold feature is typical of storytelling. However, there is no individual significance attached to any of the three references except the suggestion that there are many reasons why sown seed may fail to produce grain.

The contrasting element is that other seed falls on the good soil and bears fruit—thirtyfold, sixtyfold, and one hundredfold. Notice the threefold reference to success balancing the threefold pattern of failure. By end stress the emphasis and weight of the parable falls on this later part. In spite of the fact that there are many reasons why some seed will not produce, other seed will produce abundantly, and it is because of this fact that the sower sows.

In contemporary terms no farmer plants in order to find out the various ways in which seed can fail to produce. The farmer plants because he has confidence in an abundant harvest, but he knows that not all will yield. So in this parable the disciples feel that their work will bear abundant fruit even though not every effort will be crowned with achievement. We do not labor to find out the ways in which we might fail anymore than we engage in our occupation in order to discover the various factors that will keep us from succeeding. We work because we have confidence that some seed will bear fruit.

The allegorical interpretation obscures this positive meaning by changing the emphasis. It changes the parable of the sower into an allegory of the soils. Each of the soils represents one kind of hearer. The allegory really informs us about what to expect when we go out into the world. Instead of being a parable of faith—God's work will bear fruit in spite of the obstacles—it now shows the Christian the kinds of persons he will face, and cushions him from failure by showing that the failure is rooted in the quality of the audience. Good hearers are now only one of four kinds of people that must be faced. Luke's form makes this most evident since he records only the single positive result: "yielded a hundredfold." The major part of the allegorical interpretation, then, shows the reasons why people don't respond. While the reasons are valid and true, and hearing correctly is a significant emphasis in this Gospel, the confidence in the Christian message bearing fruit has been dulled. The preacher and the Christian are consoled by the fact that the people are hardhearted. What more could be expected? The stress on the soils dulls the confidence with which a Christian ought to proclaim the Word of God. Certainly the quality of the hearer affects the results, but the parable is not intended to describe certain types of people, rather to proclaim confidence in God's word and work. The disciple proclaims the faith in spite of obstacles, knowing there will be a harvest.

The positive orientation of the parable of the sower is illuminated by the context in which it is told in Mark and Luke. The parable is located in the early part of Jesus' ministry when the crowds are following him, and suggests the fruitfulness of proclaiming God's Word to the multitude. The teachings that immediately follow carry the same theme. "Is a lamp brought in to be put under a bushel, or under a bed, and not on a stand? For there is nothing hid, except to be made manifest; nor is anything secret, except to come to light" (Mark 4: 21–22). The veiled kingdom is to be revealed. These are strong injunctions for proclaiming the gospel with confidence. We read in Mark 4: 9, "He who has ears to hear, let him hear." The gospel is proclaimed; let men hear.

Yet, as in this parable which we are discussing, Jesus does not allow the success of the moment to blind him to the fact that not all will respond, because not all seeds find adequate soil. "Take heed how you hear; for to him who has will more be given, and from him who has not, even what he thinks that he has will be taken away (Luke 8: 18).

Only after recording the parable of the sower does Mark introduce the parables of the kingdom, disclosing to those with ears to hear the working of God's rule. But such parables are not designed to reveal how people will not respond to God; they are proclaimed so that we will heed his call. The way of the kingdom is to be made manifest in the world through the disciple who is its herald. Thus the parable of the sower and the subsequent verses give the reason for the proclamation of Jesus' message: light must be made manifest, seed exists in order to be sown, and—though God adds to the harvest—what we give greatly determines what we get.

The temptation is for the disciple to withdraw in the face of the odds, as Jesus puts it, to "light a lamp and put it under a bushel" (Matthew 5: 15). Though the darkness is vast compared to the little source of light, the light has the power. It disperses darkness far beyond its own flame. The power is with God; but in the face of the darkened and unseasoned world, the disciple is tempted to withdraw, to hide the light, to put the salt back in the cellar.

The one thing the disciple cannot do is to lose his power—"If salt has lost its taste, how shall its saltness be restored? It is no longer good for anything except to be thrown out and trodden under foot by men" (Matthew 5: 13). Seed must be sown. Not all will be harvested; but let's not keep the seed in the packet, or we will be like the man who buried his talent in the ground. Seed is not meant to be saved, but broadcast. We must not let failures keep us from sowing and reaping the harvest.

"The kingdom of heaven is like a grain of mustard seed which a man took and sowed in his field; it is the smallest of all seeds, but when it has grown it is the greatest of shrubs and becomes a tree, so that the birds of the air come and make nests in its branches." Matthew 13:31–32

"The kingdom of heaven is like leaven which a woman took and hid in three measures of meal, till it was all leavened." Matthew 13:33

Chapter Eight

RELATIONSHIPS OF THE KINGDOM

While the parables of the kingdom suggest in general terms the meaning of man's relation to God, there are certain parables that deal specifically with aspects of kingdom relationships. In these are considered the consequences of the kingdom of God in the life of the Christian disciple as he ventures forth on his own mission in the world. The ongoing work of the kingdom compels us to live by its power.

Relationship with God

The primary aspect of these relationships of the kingdom is our relationship with God.

THE PARABLE OF THE UNJUST JUDGE

The unjust judge in Luke 18:1–8 presents an arresting likeness between unlike things. The unjust judge cared neither for God's will nor for humanitarian justice. Consequently, in his self-centeredness he refused to heed the cause of the widow. Yet when she bothered him persistently he responded out of self-interest and not out of any regard for justice. In order to keep from being bothered and worn out, he said that he would heed the widow.

Now if the unrighteous judge will yield to the widow for whom he has no concern, will not God heed his own who call to him night and day? Or we might paraphrase: If such a scoundrel will heed the widow's plea, how much more will God heed his own children who beseech him?

THE PARABLE OF THE PERSISTENT FRIEND

The parable in Luke 11: 5–8 also proceeds in argument from the lesser case to the greater. The question is asked as to who in need would go to a friend asking to borrow some bread, and would be told by the friend not to bother him. The response from the listener would be one of shock. What kind of friend would answer by saying, "Do not bother me!" No one has a friend like that. This kind of action is inconceivable. The story then goes on to point out that even such an inconceivable friend would get up and grant the request for purely selfish reasons. Palestinian hospitality demanded the feeding of a guest who arrived on a journey. But here the host is caught with nothing on hand and goes to his neighbor at midnight for food so that he can meet the law of hospitality. The friend won't inconvenience himself to get up and give the host food for friendship's sake, but even he will get up when the host persists and when getting up and giving food is the only hope for further sleep. Now if such a disgusting person would grant the request of those who besought him, how much more will God, who in no way is like this friend, hear those who cry to him?

The whole message is contained in the parallel passage given later in the context, "What father among you, if his son asks for a fish, will instead of a fish give him a serpent; or if he asks for an egg, will give him a scorpion? If you then, who are evil, know how to give good gifts to your children, how much more will the heavenly Father give the Holy Spirit to those who ask him?" (Luke 11: 11–13).

Our relation to God is one of humble dependence. It is the Father who satisfies human needs. If the most unworthy men respond to human cries even for the worst motives, how much more will a good God heed the cries of those who call to him and who are dependent upon him? We are taught through the parable that we must ask, seek, and knock upon the Father's door. Rather than expressing self-centeredness, continual beseeching of the Father means dependence and surrender.

The second form of the parable in Luke 11: 11–13) specifically applies this meaning to the question of prayer. Applying the parable to prayer makes the meaning concrete, but it also limits the concept involved. Dependence is acknowledged by bringing needs to the Father in the attitude of prayer. Prayer is opening yourself to God and acknowledging that you need him. This promise of a Father who knows how to give good gifts to those who ask, does not suggest that you can get whatever you ask, but that God will give the Holy Spirit to those who ask him for it. (Compare Matthew 7: 11; notice especially "good things.") God gives that gift which is in line with his purpose, as a wise father gives his child what is good.

THE PARABLE OF THE PHARISEE AND THE PUBLICAN

The parable of the Pharisee and the publican in Luke 18: 9–14 has the specific introduction, "He also told this parable to some who trusted in themselves that they were righteous and despised others" (Luke 18: 9). The conclusion is that the humble man is exalted with God while he who exalts himself is rejected of God. It is told against the Pharisee and has the force of an example. The Pharisee does not see his life in relation to God and in dependence upon him, but rather compares himself with other men. This precludes a true relationship with God.

The Pharisee is telling the truth when he says, "I am not like other men, extortioners, unjust, adulterers, or even like this tax collector. I fast twice a week, I give tithes of all that I get" (Luke 18:11–12). Nevertheless, he is cutting himself off from God. He is a hypocrite, a playactor, because he deceives himself into thinking that his goodness is his own and that he lives on a different level of life than "this tax collector." He is no longer conscious of his dependence upon God and the miracle of new life that comes from him. Rather, he is conscious of his superiority as he compares himself with other men. He separates himself from humanity, and thereby his very goodness becomes his downfall. So he thanks God for his own goodness. Not only prayers of petition can be turned into selfish acts; this can be done even with prayers of thanksgiving.

The publican does not compare himself to any man, but stands before God conscious of the disparity between God's goodness and his own. He is acutely aware of his need, which leads him to pray, "God, be merciful to me a sinner!" (Luke 18: 13). Upon such a person God can bestow his gifts of love and forgiveness. The Pharisee could use no gifts from God, for in his own eyes he had arrived. He lived on the level of personal achievement rather than in humble dependence on the goodness of God. God could not get to him; he did not need God.

THE PARABLES OF THE TWO SONS
AND THE TWO DEBTORS

A similar contrast between dependence upon God and the feeling of self-sufficiency is made in the parables of the two sons in Matthew 21: 28–31 and the two debtors in Luke 7: 36–50. These parables criticize the Pharisees, who objected to outcasts being eligible for the grace of the kingdom. In the parable of the two debtors, Jesus is speaking in answer to the criticism of a Pharisee named Simon. This Pharisee has criticized Jesus for allowing a disreputable woman to kiss and annoint his feet. Simon reasoned that if Jesus was a prophet he should have seen what kind of woman she was, and should have withdrawn from her. In the parable of the two debtors, the Pharisee is forced to judge himself in response to Jesus' question. It is the woman who, without pretense or claims, loves the most because she has been forgiven the most. In order to love, one must know how much one has received and been forgiven.

THE PARABLE OF THE UNCLEAN SPIRIT

Closely related to these qualifications of discipleship are the sayings of Jesus that deal with the power of a God-centered life. The story of the unclean spirit in Matthew 12: 43–45 and in Luke 11: 24–26, which was cast out of its human dwelling, suggests that simply to rid our life of evil is not to achieve a Christian life. The problem is not casting out evil so much as filling life with God-centered devotion. The parable indicates that to get rid of the evil spirit only leaves a man open for a worse state than the previous one, because the multitude of evil spirits that are experiencing a housing shortage will enter if they find an empty or an uncommitted life. Luke connects this story with the preceding verse, "He who is not with me is against me, and he who does not gather with me scatters" (Luke 11: 23), which sums up the force of the whole narrative. To fail to be for God is, in effect, to be against him. There is no neutral ground. The life of the Christian disciple must be filled with positive devotion and service. Merely to abstain from evil is to succumb to evil.

Relation to Neighbor

Man is dependent upon God for his gifts. Once received, these gifts must be used and shown forth in the world. To fail to show them means that we have failed to receive them. If you have received something from the Father it must then be displayed as you live with your neighbor. Just as faith is living in relation to God, so the expression of the faith means living in a new relationship to fellowman and the world. Christian ethics is not comprised of striving to keep rules, but of entering into relationship with all. Such relationship is determined not by rules but by the understanding and care that enables all involved to grow within it.

THE PARABLE OF THE UNFORGIVING SERVANT

The parable on forgiveness (see Matthew 18: 23–35) is an example rather than a striking contrast of unlike things. The king forgave the servant a large debt; but the servant refused to forgive his own debtor a small debt, and had him cast into prison. The unforgiving servant was then delivered to the tormentors until his debt should be paid in full. The force of the whole story is that we shall forgive even as we have been forgiven, and the application is made in these words, "So also my heavenly Father will do to every one of you, if you do not forgive your brother from your heart" (Matthew 18: 35). We must live by the forgiveness we have received. This reveals vividly that failure to live by God's gift is to lose that gift and to bring ourself under his judgment. The judgment of God is not of the sort that says: "Be good and then you shall be rewarded." God gives his grace freely. But he does insist that if we would possess these gifts, we must manifest their fruits and live by them. To fail to act responsibly is to bring judgment upon ourself.

The size of the debt suggests how much more the servant was forgiven than he was called on to forgive. The debt of the forgiven servant had been incredibly large. Josephus suggests that Herod the Great's total income for a year was 900 talents compared to a debt listed here as 10,000 talents. The forgiven servant is obviously no menial laborer, but a financier. He owes over ten times the national budget. The size of the debt is incredible, and drives home the point of the parable by its contrast with the paltry amount the servant refuses to forgive. Here the vividness and force of the parable are derived from the great contrast between the figures.

The story of the good Samaritan also deals with man's relation to his neighbor. It does not deal with forgiveness, but with the closely related attitude of love, out of which neighborly action naturally grows. Love is not a vague sentiment or feeling, but it is an expressive action. You will notice that this parable does not define "my neighbor," that instead, it describes the neighborly man. (Compare Luke 10: 29–36.) We must not think of the word *neighbor* as meaning someone else; rather, we must realize that we are the neighbor whose concern must extend to anyone who is in need. The motive comes from understanding our own being. We are the disciple! We are the neighbor!

Understanding Oneself

The disciple not only needs a right understanding of his relation to God and neighbor but a correct understanding of himself as well.

THE PARABLE OF THE UNWORTHY SERVANT

In the parable of the unworthy servant (Luke 17: 7–10), when the servant has finished his chores in the field he is not praised and told to rest, but is given a new job in the household. You do not thank a man for doing his duty, nor does the servant expect praise. We might paraphrase the parable by more modern terms: an employer does not thank his workers and tell them to take a vacation when they have done a job for which they were paid; rather, he keeps them busy by giving them a new job. They are not praised, because they have only done their duty.

So we—when we understand ourselves—do not see ourselves as meriting praise or honor from God for our service as if it were a voluntary or optional thing. We have only done what was demanded of us. "We are unworthy servants; we have only done what was our duty" (Luke 17: 10).

The recognition of this fact keeps us from the moral complacency and self-satisfaction of the Pharisee. If religion were a matter of human achievement and of keeping the law, there would be pride in attainment. But we are dependent upon God. God owns all since he has given all. All that we do is to make use of what God gives us, and God expects the fruit of what he has given. (Compare the parable of the talents where God expects more than was given.) We are unworthy servants. Nobody fusses over a servant when he does a day's work. In application of the parable we might say: There is no reason to expect a compliment for fulfilling our Christian responsibilities or to get huffy when we are not thanked. When we recognize that we are dependent upon God for his gifts, and when we see the necessity of being a good neighbor, there is no danger of an attitude of pride in achievement. God is the Source of our being, and he gains the glory. Serving others is not a voluntary matter that deserves praise. It is necessary that we help the needy in order to express our relationship with God. Self-discipline in serving God and others becomes a natural expression of a God-filled life.

PLACES AT TABLE

The parable of places at table (Luke 14: 7–10) reflects the same basic orientation as that of the unworthy servant. When invited to a marriage feast the invited guest takes the lowest place. If there is any honor to be bestowed, it will be given by the host. He gives the honor and he "who exalts himself will be humbled, but he who humbles himself will be exalted." True exaltation lies in recognizing dependence. God gives the place of honor and we had better not be in the position of presuming to tell God whom he must honor. The gifts belong to God.

The parable of places at table is told against the Pharisees who, believing in a religion of merit and achievement, feel that they have kept themselves pure from external taints and sins. Therefore, they assume the chief seats of honor. "They love the place of honor at feasts and the chief seats in the synagogues" (Matthew 23: 6).

The Parable About That Which Defiles

Finally, our lives are lived out of inner resources that become available by placing God at the center of life. It is not what is outside that purifies or defiles us, but what issues out of the heart. (Compare Mark 7: 14–23.) What comes out of us reveals our true character. A God-filled life has within it the resources to do the will of God. Only that can come out which has already entered and embraced the heart. It is the good tree that bears fruit (see Matthew 7: 17–20), and the fruit that a tree bears inevitably becomes the means of evaluating the tree. "You will know them by their fruits. . . . Every tree that does not bear good fruit is cut down and thrown into the fire" (Matthew 7: 16, 19).

The significance of our lives issues out of inner character, which is developed and nourished by our relation to God. It is the good tree that produces good fruit. It is not good fruit that makes a tree good, for the tree produces the fruit.

Yet this emphasis on the fruit does not negate in any way the humble confession, "We are unworthy servants." Since the fruit is the product of the tree or the expression of the inner relation to God, then it is out of the relation with God himself that the fruit is produced.

Desirable qualities for a life of discipleship may be summarized as humble dependence and devoted self-surrender, forgiveness and love, self-discipline and inner integrity.

The Relation to Possessions

An overwhelming number of the parables and sayings of Jesus are taken from the sphere of finance and the use of money. Often these parables are not on the subject of money, but have used it as an example for setting forth the kingdom of God. The parable of the talents has nothing to do with interest or interest rates in its application. It has to do with the larger question of man's responsibility to God. The parable of the laborers in the vineyard has nothing to do with paychecks, but deals with the larger questions of God's way of giving to and dealing with man. The parables are not pieces of moral advice on financial matters.

Yet the parables have far greater consequences for the use of material and financial possessions than if they were on this subject alone. Any parable that discusses man's responsibility to God inevitably has consequences for the use of the material world. Every parable that deals with the free gift of God's kingdom suggests, as part of its application, that we must not deal with our neighbor on a financial basis alone. If the gift is given us apart from merit, can we feel that financial reward for work done is the sole basis for distributing money among men? If Jesus teaches, as he does, that God demands absolute loyalty since he is King and absolute Ruler, then possessions, at best, become only tools for serving God, and can never be allowed to become a passion of our lives.

THE RICH FOOL

Because every aspect of our relation to and dependence upon God has implications for man's use of the things of the world, it is not surprising that some of the teachings of Jesus have direct application to this subject. In Luke 12: 16–21 the parable of the rich fool is used to illustrate the statement, "beware of all covetousness; for a man's life does not consist in the abundance of his possessions" (Luke 12: 15). The person who seeks to prepare for abundance in terms of wealth and the luxury that it brings has founded his existence on a very precarious base. The concluding comment is "So is he who lays up treasure for himself, and is not rich toward God."

This statement recalls the attitude toward riches expressed in the verses in the Sermon on the Mount that contrasts treasures on earth and treasures in heaven (compare Matthew 6: 19–21), and which explain that one cannot serve both God and mammon (compare Matthew 6: 24).

The parable of the dishonest steward has had affixed to it many teachings on the use of wealth. (See Luke 16: 9–13.) The original context of these sayings has been forgotten, probably because it is not necessary or relevant for understanding them. All of the sayings deal with the question of possessions. This seems to be the basis for their being included here, since the parable was about debts. Collecting sayings that dealt with the illustrative symbol, wealth, provided a convenient memory device for understanding the proper use of possessions.

"And I tell you, make friends for yourselves by means of unrighteous mammon, so that when it fails they may receive you into the eternal habitations" (Luke 16: 9) implies that the way money is used does have a crucial consequence for our destiny. Unrighteous mammon does not suggest that money is evil, but has the force of our phrase, "filthy lucre." Filthy lucre rightly used can be a means of laying up treasures in heaven.

"He who is faithful in a very little is faithful also in much; and he who is dishonest in a very little is dishonest also in much" (Luke 16: 10) suggests that man is tested in little things before he is entrusted with much. Man doesn't change character because of the amount involved. If he can cut the corner in little things, he can cut it in big things.

"If then you have not been faithful in the unrighteous mammon, who will entrust to you the true riches?" (Luke 16: 11), is another separate saying that inquires as to who will entrust you with handling the greater riches of God if you haven't been trustworthy previously in handling money. This point is reminiscent of the requirement of bishops in the early church—to handle the family of God one had to prove himself by showing that he could handle his own household. (See 1 Timothy 3: 4–5.) "And if you have not been faithful in that which is another's, who will give you that which is your own?" (Luke 16: 12) implies that if disciples can't be trusted in handling another's concern, God will not entrust them with his kingdom that is meant to be theirs. Finally, the contradictory claims between God and mammon are set forth in Luke 16: 13.

Go Thou and Do Likewise

Three of the best known parables of Jesus—the unforgiving servant, the Pharisee and the publican, and the good Samaritan—do not fit into the specific terms of the parable as a metaphorical story. We must bear in mind that the word *parable* in its Hebrew roots referred to many different kinds of narratives and figures of speech. (See chapter 2.) These three stories are examples that delineate the general approach to life that is required of us. The parables of the unforgiving servant, and the Pharisee and the publican, which are concerned with this general approach to life, have already been discussed. In these Jesus has given concrete pictures of the life required of the disciple. Yet, as in all parables, there is an extreme and unexpected contrast in the story that not only compels by example but strikes to the very heart.

These three stories set forth examples that make clear God's action and his expectations of those who would follow him. They become vivid by containing an extreme contrast with wrong action. The man forgiven a huge debt won't forgive a little one; the Pharisee boasts in his prayer while the publican humbles himself; the religious authorities (priest and Levite) pass by while the "no-good" Samaritan cares. This kind of story is especially designed to indicate expected patterns of human behavior, and best exemplifies some of the qualities of the life of the disciple—neighborliness, humility, and forgiveness. It is significant that this kind of story example is used solely where human behavior is concerned. Jesus never uses exemplars to describe God's action; this would be a comparison containing degrees of unlikeness. "If you then, who are evil, know how to give good gifts to your children, how much more will the heavenly Father give the Holy Spirit to those who ask him?" (Luke 11: 13).

THE PARABLE OF THE GOOD SAMARITAN

All three of these stories present moral examples. The story of the good Samaritan ends with the words, "Go and do likewise" (Luke 10: 37). Such a remark would be inconceivable after those parables in which unlike things are compared rather than a living example given. The characteristics of these stories fit very closely into what might be called *illustrations*. The real life setting in the story of the good Samaritan is preserved. (See Luke 10: 29–37.) A lawyer stands up to question Jesus. (See Luke 10: 25–28.) The questioner, however, is not sincere because he does not want to know the answer to the question; rather, he wants to put Jesus to the test. He is not concerned with knowing eternal life, but with discovering what kind of teacher Jesus is—can he meet the test? In such a situation Jesus, as he often does, answers with a counter-question. By this device he draws the truth from the seeker and keeps the questioner from being able to judge him. It is now the questioner who is being put on the spot. When the lawyer answers rightly from his knowledge of the Scriptures, Jesus commends the capable answer with the words, "Do this, and you will live" (Luke 10: 28).

In this remark Jesus suggests that the answer in itself is not sufficient. The answer, "You shall love the Lord your God . . . and your neighbor as yourself" (Luke 10: 27), has to be lived. A scholarly knowledge of the truth is not adequate;

97

it must be a living knowledge. The lawyer, in wanting to debate the theological questions, has avoided the crucial issue in the gospel—that of responding to the revelation and action of God. Talk of religion is easily confused with serving God. Jesus will not let the lawyer succumb to that dodge. Nor will he allow us to do so. Religious discussion groups can become an escape from meeting the judgment of God face to face. Pious questions, the desire to secure more viewpoints, the urge to make our definitions accurate, might only be a way to avoid the necessity for action.

The lawyer, now aware that he is being judged and wanting to justify his previous behavior, asks a second question, "Who is my neighbor?" (Luke 10: 29). Again his question is not for knowledge but in order to defend his actions. Nevertheless, the ground has shifted. Christ is not being judged, he has become the judge; the questioner is in the place where he has to defend not his answers, but his action.

Jesus now replies to the question, "Who is my neighbor?" not with another counter-question, since the ground of the question has been shifted, but with a story. The story also has the effect of not permitting the lawyer to judge Jesus' statement; rather, it forces the hearer to make a judgment upon the worth of the second question. The story forces the lawyer to answer his own question because it paints the issue in crystal clear terms. Because it forces its own answer the story gets the hearer to judge himself, under, of course, the supervision of the teller of the story.

Jesus then concludes the conversation with the simple statement, "Go and do likewise" (Luke 10: 37). The hearer has recognized the truth of the matter; now he goes forth to live it. In the whole incident Jesus carefully avoids getting pulled into a discussion of the matter under question. The discussion group technique was not only not his, but carefully evaded by him. The scribes loved to debate the intricate questions of the law and to test one another by their discussion. Jesus gave a call to action and to life. The faith must be known in life rather than on the level of discussion.

Since this parable is a clear illustration, little comment needs to be made about it except to remind the reader that it is told against the priest and the Levite, who share the idea that religion means avoiding contact with impure people. It is the Samaritan, an outsider, who proves to be the neighborly man by breaking through the natural antipathy between Samaritan and Jew. In this feature the parable possesses its potent and classic power, for it recognizes the service and action of the Samaritan as worth more than all the pious talk of the lawyer who asks the question. Remember that the lawyer or scribe was a student of the religious or Hebrew law. He was the professional theologian.

THE PARABLE OF THE FOUNDATIONS

A parable that gives a summary or concluding tone to the question of discipleship ends the Sermon on the Mount. (See Matthew 7: 24–27.) Life can be built on two different foundations. The foundations on which life is built are as crucial as the difference between rock and sand for the foundation of a house. In the parable, the difference is not in the houses; each is just as much a house. Nor is the difference between the materials out of which the house was built (as in "The Three Little Pigs"). The sole difference is in the foundation on which the house was built, which became discernible only when the testing floods came. To hear God's will and to live by it is to build upon the rock.

In Luke 6: 46–49 there is a slight variation in that the wise builder "dug deep" and laid the foundation on the rock. The house was "well built." The foolish builder proceeded "without a foundation." Luke stresses the diligence of the builder rather than the foundation alone.

He also told this parable to some who trusted in themselves that they were righteous and despised others: "Two men went up into the temple to pray, one a Pharisee and the other a tax collector. The Pharisee stood and prayed thus with himself, 'God, I thank thee that I am not like other men, extortioners, unjust, adulterers, or even like this tax collector. I fast twice a week, I give tithes of all that I get.' But the tax collector, standing far off, would not even lift up his eyes to heaven, but beat his breast, saying, 'God, be merciful to me a sinner!' I tell you, this man went down to his house justified rather than the other; for every one who exalts himself will be humbled, but he who humbles himself will be exalted."

Luke 18: 9–14

Chapter Nine

THE WAY OF GOD AND THE WAY OF MAN

Some of the parables of Jesus compare and contrast the manner of both divine and human activity. Frequently they note the difference between the way of God and the way of man. Always they compel us to consider the supreme way of the Father.

God and the Sinner

Three parables in the fifteenth chapter of Luke were addressed to the scribes and Pharisees when the tax collectors and sinners drew near to Jesus. The remark, "This man receives sinners and eats with them" (Luke 15: 2) is the setting given to these parables. They are Jesus' answer to the criticism of his relation to outcasts, and are directed against the egotistical ideas of religious purity held by the keepers of the law.

THE PARABLE OF THE LOST SHEEP

The parable of the lost sheep in Luke 15: 3–7 answers the Pharisees' criticism with the affirmation that God is like the shepherd who searches after the lost sheep until he finds it. The parable points out how the shepherd leaves the ninety-nine to go after the lost one, rejoicing when he finds it and calling the neighbors in to celebrate. The force lies in the line, "There will be more joy in heaven over one sinner who

101

repents than over ninety-nine righteous persons who need no repentance" (Luke 15:7). This radical image expresses God's great joy over a recovered sinner. The answer to the scribes' accusation, "This man receives sinners and eats with them" (Luke 15:2) is acceptance of it. This is how God is. The parable presents no example of repentance. It is an affirmation of God's character, rather than a treatise on repentance. Such a claim about God is a shock to the Pharisees. Whether this idea fits the Pharisees' criteria of logic and fair play or not, God rejoices over the lost who are recovered.

THE PARABLE OF THE LOST COIN

The companion parable of the lost coin in Luke 15: 8–10, similarly does not deal with repentance, but with the nature of God. The woman searches diligently for the lost coin. The extent of her search only makes the joy greater when it is found. As in the previous parable, such joy is too great to be kept to oneself. Immediately the woman goes forth to tell her neighbors. In both parables joy is pictured as something that man must inevitably share with others. Joy has an inner dynamism that carries its expression to all around. It bubbles forth. So God also rejoices over the recovered sinner.

THE PARABLE OF THE PRODIGAL SON

In the parable of the prodigal son in Luke 15: 11–32, the issue again is not repentance. The climax of the story is the joy of the father—not the repentance of the son. When the father sees his prodigal son he runs to him and kisses and embraces him compassionately before the son can utter his repentance. While the son sets forth his unworthiness, the father decorates him and prepares a feast for his recovery.

This parable is different from the two preceding it, however, in that a new note is introduced at this point. The elder brother, who has always been faithful to family dignity, has never received such a feast. "You have never fussed over me," he complains in effect. By his logic this attitude toward the prodigal is unfair. The contrast between the joy of the father and the jealousy of the elder brother is emphasized. Such a parable, if told to the Pharisees as suggested in Luke, chapter 15, is a direct retort to their jealous questioning of Jesus' concern over the sinner. While the first two parables presented the joy of recovering the lost, here the moral worthlessness of what was lost comes into play, making what might seem to be the unfairness of the father's reaction, evident. The action toward the prodigal makes the case of the elder brother seem unfair.

Perhaps the climax of the answer to the elder son is in the line, "Son, you are always with me, and all that is mine is yours" (Luke 15: 31). The elder son has no need of jealousy. Although a feast has never been made for him, all that is the father's is his. He has not suffered any separation. He is one with the owner. In a sense he is the owner giving the feast, not one who has been neglected or overlooked by members of the household.

The Oriental sense of community that is lacking in the West is the evident basis of this parable. The father and the son have shared all things. There has been no wronging of the elder son, no rejection of him. Good relationships with other people are not characterized by social feasting, but by continual community. Such relationships do not depend on making merry, as is befitting the restoration of what had been lost.

It is these words of the father in verse 31 that make the tragedy of the brother's misconception more apparent, because the brother has not recognized the basic character of his relation to the father. He has not understood the continuous and shared character of their communion. Although he was included in his father's joy—they had been together constantly and he had reason to rejoice with his father—his reply indicated the separation that existed in his own mind,

103

DICK LEBOWITZ

The way of the God of reconciling love sometimes shines out of the expressions of young people

*Men, on the other hand, can practically breathe
into one another's faces, yet be millions of miles apart*

"Lo, these many years I have served you, and I never disobeyed your command; yet you never gave me a kid, that I might make merry with my friends" (Luke 15:29). It is *I* and *you*, never *we*. This alone shows that the elder son has not seen that "All that is mine is yours," but really thinks of himself as separated from the father and the object of his actions, rather than belonging to the father and being the participant and coauthor of his deeds. With such a conception of his relation to his father the elder son cannot comprehend that he shares in the joy of the father. This not only keeps him from enjoying the feast but also, by his separating himself, makes him think that his father must do things for him as if he were separate.

This is finally and clearly indicated in the words, "But when this son of yours came, who has devoured your living with harlots, you killed for him the fatted calf" (Luke 15:30). The elder son has cut *himself* off from the father and the family and in so doing cannot participate in the joy of the father.

The parable contrasts the joy of the father with the jealousy of the elder brother—jealousy that is rooted in the elder brother's own failure to understand his relationship to the father. It is just like when a co-owner in a business throws a banquet honoring an employee. This is not an occasion for the other owner to feel slighted. Actually, he is giving the feast too, for he is a partner and should share equally in the joy as well as in the benefits. When we apply the parable to the modern church member rather than to the Pharisee, we can easily see how often the active member is insulted like the elder brother when a new convert is honored, given office, or praised. He responds, "I've belonged to this church all these years but they never did that for me." There you have it—*they* and *me*—the elder brother exactly. The church member cuts himself off from the church and its God. He reveals that he does not understand the nature of the church. In reality, the church member is giving the feast. He hasn't been left out—he is one with the host.

Yet, in the story of the prodigal we cannot forget that the lost item is a person who shared a responsibility for his decision. The son has laid claim to his share of the family inheritance. In modern terms we would say, "He sought his freedom and independence." He did not want the feeling of obligation to his family. But in destroying his roots and cutting himself off from his home he was doomed to failure. The kind of freedom he sought—the desire to do as he pleased, without responsibility—meant a life of self-destruction and its consequent self-degradation. To seek oneself is to lose oneself: "For whoever would save his life will lose it" (Matthew 16: 25 and Mark 8: 35).

What promised freedom did not actually bring freedom at all. It resulted in self-destruction that meant slavery, and was that kind of pseudo-freedom we so often seek in the world today—away from the Father. When the prodigal cut himself off from the father, what looked like independence meant destruction. What looked like freedom meant slavery. Evil always wears a tempting and appealing garment.

Can we escape this humiliation? There is one way—to return to the Father. More than a sheep or a coin, which correspondingly stray or are misplaced through no fault of their own, could ever be lost, the prodigal is lost and forlorn. He made the choice that led to his wretched state; he also chose to return to that which he had rejected. What he discovered in his own experience of judgment was that we find true freedom in our Father's house. In Paul's terms the choice lies between being sons of God or being slaves. As sons we have privileges in our Father's house. We have the free run of the house; we share all things with the Father, for we are one family. When the prodigal took his small portion of the property he gave up the real inheritance: the fact that all that is the father's is the son's as long as they are one. As the elder brother, but in his own way, he had failed to know the meaning of true communion. *Freedom* means to acknowledge dependence upon the Father and to live with him and to be able to freely use all that is his.

God shares all that is his with us; and we can share with him all that is ours—our cares, our troubles, our sins. To be responsible to the Father is to be free from worry, from the fear of failure, from the power of sin and its destruction. The Father eagerly awaits those who will return to him and gain freedom.

God and His Miracles

A second comparison and contrast of the way of God and the way of man included in the parables is in the area of God and his miracles.

THE PARABLE OF THE RICH MAN AND LAZARUS

This comparison and contrast of the way of God and the way of man in the area of miracles is contained in the parable of the rich man and Lazarus. (See Luke 16: 19–31.) This is an extensive parable in which the positions of the rich man and Lazarus are reversed following their death. The rich man is now in hades and Lazarus is in Abraham's bosom. When the rich man becomes aware that his life has been ill spent, he pleads with Abraham to send Lazarus to warn his five brothers in order that they might not come to the same end. They, too, lack the sight to see God at work on earth. But in the parable Abraham replies, "They have Moses and the prophets; let them hear them" (Luke 16: 29). That is, they have the Scriptures. ("Moses" and "the prophets" were names of the two parts of scripture in Jesus' day, and they referred to the five books of the law and the eight books of the prophets that were accepted.) The rich man answers, however, that his brothers will not respond to the Scriptures

108

and repent. The assumption in the rich man's answer is that while men will not respond to the preaching of God's word, they will respond to the stupendous and the miraculous—if God would only cause a miracle, then men would respond.

Abraham replies, "If they do not hear Moses and the prophets, neither will they be convinced if some one should rise from the dead" (Luke 16: 31). If we will not respond to the word and will of God, says the narrative, neither will we respond to the stupendous. The miraculous is not a means by which faith can be secured. In fact it is just the opposite. It is only the man of belief who can see the working of God in its mysterious and hidden aspect. Only he can see the miraculous. Faith enables us to see the hand of God at work in the world. Such a vision is impossible without faith. The understanding of the miraculous flows from faith; it does not create faith. Or to paraphrase the words of Jesus, "It is faith that moves mountains"; but modern man tends to reverse the statement and say to God, "Move the mountains and then I will believe." If the miraculous created faith, then the basic teaching of Jesus about the kingdom—that its working now is veiled and it takes eyes to see and ears to hear—would be destroyed.

Men would have God convince the world of his presence and power by proof in terms of stupendous eruptions in the order of the world. Men dislike a kingdom whose way is veiled, whose gate is narrow and hard to discern, and that demands eyes to see and ears to hear. Yet this is the kingdom that God has given, and men will have to accept it on God's terms. God does not prove himself by violating the order that he has created. God does not work against himself. But for those with eyes to see, God's action is manifest as he rules his order and directs it according to his purpose. Yet these wonderful ways and mysteries of God are known only to the ear that hears the word of God with *faith*.

"Or what woman, having ten silver coins, if she loses one coin, does not light a lamp and sweep the house and seek diligently until she finds it? And when she has found it, she calls together her friends and neighbors, saying, 'Rejoice with me, for I have found the coin which I had lost.' Even so, I tell you, there is joy before the angels of God over one sinner who repents."

Luke 15: 8–10

Chapter Ten

JESUS IN THE PARABLES

This subject might well have been the opening chapter because it is crucial to the Christian faith. Yet the disciples themselves did not realize the place of Jesus in the kingdom until they realized the power of God as it already worked in their lives. They were then forced to ask themselves who it was that brought the rule of God into their lives.

Since it is in this final chapter that we consider the place of Jesus in relation to the kingdom, we must not conclude that the disciples knew the kingdom of God apart from the reality and the power of Jesus as the Christ—that in later years they began to wonder about Jesus, and eventually carved a niche for him in the kingdom which they had already experienced without him. The kingdom was known only through the works and person of Jesus. He brought the kingdom to the disciples; he was not fitted into it after his death. According to the testimony of the Gospels, there would have been no experience of the kingdom without Jesus. When Jesus taught, the demand of the kingdom was real; men had to follow or not. When he acted, his action brought men into a new relationship with God. The rule of God became real in all that he did. He was the touchstone of the kingdom of God.

The story of the father's love in the parable of the prodigal son would have been a laugh if men had not already begun to experience such love through Jesus. After all, it was the fact that he ate with tax collectors and sinners (see Luke 15:2) that gave rise to the need for the story; and Jesus, as we pointed out in the previous chapter, merely accepted the Pharisees' cold-hearted accusation. The proclamation of God's unlimited forgiveness would have been irrelevant if men had not already begun to know that forgiveness in Jesus. The demand of the kingdom would have been an idle tale had not men felt his claim upon their lives. What Jesus proclaimed, men experienced in him. He was the Word incarnate.

The New and the Old

The Gospels proclaim that in the life of Jesus a new dimension has been added to man's experience of God.

CHILDREN IN THE MARKET PLACE

In Matthew 11: 16–19 the response of the populace to both Jesus and John is compared to the seemingly unrelated situation of grumbling children. Part of the children want to play music so that their playmates can dance, but the others refuse. So they suggest playing funeral, but again their playmates refuse. Just as most fickle children aren't satisfied with any suggestion, so that generation grumbled when John came fasting, saying, "He has a demon" (Matthew 11: 18). But when Jesus came he was called "a glutton and a drunkard, a friend of tax collectors and sinners" (Matthew 11: 19). Both John and Jesus were God's messengers, but men hate both the message of repentance and the proclamation of the feast of the kingdom. They grumble. "Yet wisdom is justified by her deeds" (Matthew 11: 19). In this whole discussion it is evident that these two in a unique way have brought the activity of God to new reality. This inevitably raises the question, What relation does the new element in the revelation of God have to the old?

PARABLE ABOUT THE UNPATCHED GARMENT

A parable directly related to this question of the relation of the new element to the old in the revelation of God is the parable of the unpatched garment. (See Matthew 9:16; Mark 2:21; and Luke 5:36.) No one is foolish enough to patch an old garment with a new cloth. This folly was more obvious in the days before fabrics were preshrunk because on the first washing the new fabrics in the patch would shrink and consequently tear the old material worse than if it had not been patched at all.

The implication of this parabolic analogy is that the old religion cannot be patched up with the new experiences. The consequence would only be of harm to the old. There is an incompatibility between the new and the old. To accommodate the new to the old without venturing forth is virtually an impossibility.

The form of this parable in Mark 2:21 differs from that in Luke 5:36. The reason given in Luke 5:36 for refusing to patch the old garment is twofold: (1) A new garment will have to be torn to get the new material. (2) The new material will not match the old. The reasons given in Luke are much more prosaic and have lost their arresting character. Consequently, the form of the parable in Luke does not require the parabolic style.

THE PARABLE ABOUT NEW WINE IN OLD WINESKINS

A second parable is also concerned with the relation between the new and the old forms of religion—the parable about new wine in old wineskins. (See Matthew 9:17; Mark 2:22; and Luke 5:37–39.) New wine still will ferment and bubble up—it has potency. If it is made in old skins that are brittle, the vitality of the wine will crack the semirigid and hardened skins, and both the wine and the skins will be lost. New wine has to be made with fresh skins that are pliable, and that can respond to and stretch with the potency and seething of the contents.

This parable suggests that the old forms of life and religion do not have the resilience to contain the potency and

113

The kingdom of God is known only
through the works and person of Jesus

vitality of the new spirit. New forms and institutions must be devised to enable the new wine of the spirit to be expressed without losing both the old forms and the new power. To try to channel it in the old ways means only to lose both. New power requires new vehicles of communication. In Luke an additional saying of Jesus is added to the parable of new wine in old wineskins. It, too, uses a saying about wine as the means for illustrating the point. It seems to reveal man's resistance to receiving the new. Man prefers the staid and traditional. He doesn't like to venture with the new. "No one after drinking old wine desires new; . . . 'The old is good' " (Luke 5:39).

The context given to the three sayings so far presented in this chapter has to do with the question of why the disciples of Jesus do not fast like the disciples of John. The answer of the parables is that the gospel cannot be contained in the old practices of Judaism. Luke 5:39 clearly explains why the disciples of John continue and do not recognize the superiority of the new. It later offers the church an insight into the failure of Christian evangelism. Man by nature sticks to the old.

TREASURES NEW AND OLD

A final saying equates the scribe of the kingdom to a householder who brings out of his treasures what is new and what is old. He is neither conservative nor a faddist. (See Matthew 13:52.) Benjamin W. Bacon remarks that the author of Matthew accomplished this by combining a rich use of the Old Testament heritage with the new leaven of the gospel.[7]

Connected with these ideas in the teaching of Jesus is the sense that with his ministry something new has happened. The old order has given way to the new. This is implied, in part, in the parable of the marriage feast (see Mark 2: 18–20) which precedes the parable of the unshrunk garment. Jesus is questioned as to why his disciples do not fast when the disciples of John and the Pharisees fast. The answer suggests that even as wedding celebrations are the time for feasting, the presence of Jesus has brought a new reality into being. The feast of the kingdom is here and has replaced the fast of preparation. But what is Jesus' place in the kingdom if it is through his activity that it is inaugurated? The relation of the new and the old is inevitably bound up first and last with the question: Who is Jesus?

Jesus and John the Baptist

A central question the Gospels face is the relation between Jesus and John the Baptist. When the Baptist inquires, "Are you he who is to come, or shall we look for another?" (Matthew 11: 2), Jesus replies by calling John's attention to the works that he does. He then proceeds to indicate his deep regard for the work of John the Baptist. "Among those born of women there has risen no one greater than John the Baptist; yet he who is least in the kingdom of heaven is greater than he" (Matthew 11: 11). John and the old order which he climaxes are great, and yet something new has been introduced. The result is that even the one who is least in the new order is greater than John.

A parabolic statement that is very difficult to interpret then follows. "From the days of John the Baptist until now the kingdom of heaven suffered violence, and men of violence take it by force" (Matthew 11: 12). The statement can mean that since John the Baptist the evil forces recognizing that the kingdom has come have been subjecting the kingdom to attack, seeking to destroy it in its incipient stages; or it can mean that since the days of John, the kingdom has come and men eagerly seek and grasp its opportunities. In either case it is evident that the kingdom has come subsequent to the work of John. This applies whether evil seeks to destroy it or whether eager men aggressively grasp for its benefits. The power of God unfolds decisively in Jesus.

116

Acted Parables of Jesus

A number of the decisive actions of Jesus that reveal his own crucial position are like acted parables, such as the triumphal entry (the king is a figure of meekness and lowliness, not the expected David), the cleansing of the temple (Christ is the inaugurator of a new worship which replaces that of the temple and its mediating priesthood), and the Lord's Supper (the new covenant of communion with a Lord who has given his body and blood in suffering service for his disciples has replaced the covenant of the loyalty to the law).

The Kingdom of God and the Kingdom of Evil

Another facet of the kingdom that directly involves the person of Jesus is the conflict between the kingdom of God and the kingdom of evil.

SATAN CASTING OUT SATAN

In the conflict between two kingdoms Jesus plays a central role. In the parable of Satan casting out Satan, Jesus says: "If a kingdom is divided against itself, that kingdom cannot stand. And if a house is divided against itself, that house will not be able to stand. And if Satan has risen up against himself and is divided, he cannot stand, but is coming to an end" (Mark 3: 23–26). The direct conflict between the works of Jesus and the kingdom of evil is set forth. This parable is told in answer to the charge that Jesus casts out demons because he is in the employ of the chief of the demons. Jesus' answer shows that if he casts out demons he is the inevitable antagonist of the power of evil. Not only is he the antagonist, but he goes on to imply that his work is to bind the evil one. "But no one can enter a strong man's house and plunder his goods, unless he first binds the strong man; then indeed he may plunder his house" (Mark 3: 27).

JESUS IN THE PARABLES

THE UNCLEAN SPIRIT

In the parable of the unclean spirit in Matthew 12: 43–45, the casting out of evil is pictured as part of the conflict with the new age, although it is made patently clear that the mere casting out of evil in no way brings in the new kingdom. The casting out of evil is one of the signs of the kingdom, since the coming of the kingdom of God brings inevitable conflict with the kingdom of evil.

The Exorcisms of Jesus

While not belonging to the parables, Jesus' exorcisms (healings in which he casts out demons) illuminate the meaning expressed in the parable of Satan casting out Satan. In the healing ministry of Jesus the attack against the kingdom of evil has begun. Demons may resist, but they must eventually acknowledge their master. In Jesus' action the kingdom of God has launched its offensive against the forces of evil.

Jesus, Friend of Tax Collectors and Sinners

Not only has the kingdom of God attacked the kingdom of evil in the person of Jesus, but the conflict between God and human sin has reached its focus in him. When Jesus is accused of eating with tax collectors and sinners he responds with the parable, "Those who are well have no need of a physician, but those who are sick. . . . I came not to call the righteous, but sinners" (Matthew 9: 12–13).

In Luke 7: 36–50 the parable of the two debtors is part of a larger discussion in which the subject is the relation between forgiveness and love. When accused of receiving favors from a woman of ill repute, Jesus responds by telling of the two debtors—one who was forgiven much, and the other little. Then Jesus asks the question, "Now which of them will love him more?" (Luke 7: 42). By this question he appeals to the insight and self-discovery of his Pharisaic critic Simon, and in so doing gets him to condemn himself. The answer shows that it is the woman who was forgiven much, who loved her master and showed him hospitality—not the Pharisee who saw little need for his own forgiveness. "Therefore I tell you, her sins, which are many, are forgiven, for she loved much; but he who is forgiven little, loves little" (Luke 7: 47). This verse must not be misunderstood. Love is not the condition of forgiveness here, but the expression of its reality. The limitation on forgiveness is not imposed by God, but by the view that the man has of himself.

In Jesus the new power of the gospel is at work—work that other forms of religion cannot contain or express; the kingdom of evil is now constantly under attack, and is being bound by the onslaught of Jesus; the sin that attempts to rule us is being overcome in forgiveness and love by the physician of the heart.

In the working of the kingdom of God, the parables have the potential of enabling the Word of God to erupt into our lives—an eruption that holds us responsible for hearing.

Acknowledgments

CHAPTER ONE

1. Willard H. Robinson, *The Parables of Jesus* (University of Chicago Press, 1928), p. 11. Used by permission of the University of Chicago Press.
2. C. H. Dodd, *The Parables of the Kingdom* (Charles Scribner's Sons, New York, 1961, revised edition), pp. 1–2. Used by permission of Charles Scribner's Sons and James Nisbet & Co., Ltd.

CHAPTER TWO

1. Archibald M. Hunter, *Interpreting the Parables* (Westminster Press, Philadelphia, 1960), p. 11.
2. Ernest Cadman Colwell, *An Approach to the Teaching of Jesus* (Abingdon Press, Nashville, 1947), p. 27. Used by permission.
3. Walter Russell Bowie, "The Parables" in *The Interpreter's Bible* (Abingdon Press, Nashville, 1951), vol. 7, p. 167.
4. Joachim Jeremias, *The Parables of Jesus* (Charles Scribner's Sons, New York, 1955), pp. 13–16.

CHAPTER FOUR

1. Helmut Thielicke, *The Waiting Father* (Copyright by John W. Doberstein, 1959), pp. 122–123. Used by permission of Harper & Row Publishers, New York.

CHAPTER FIVE

1. *Ibid.*, p. 63.

CHAPTER SEVEN

1. John Bunyan, *Pilgrim's Progress* (Rinehart & Co., Inc., New York, 1949), p. 70.

2. H. D. A. Major, T. W. Manson, and C. J. Wright, *The Mission and Message of Jesus*. (E. P. Dutton and Co., Inc, New York, 1938), p. 584.

CHAPTER TEN

1. Benjamin W. Bacon, *Studies in Matthew* (Henry Holt & Co., New York, 1930), p. 131.

Appendix

Alphabetical Listing of the Parables
(including biblical references and page numbers)

Barren Fig Tree, *Luke 13: 6–9*, **35, 62**

Budding Fig Tree, The, *Mark 13: 28; Matt. 24: 32*, **15, 66**

Burglar, The, *Luke 12: 39–40; Matt. 24: 43–44*, **60**

Children in the Marketplace, The, *Matt. 11: 16–19; Luke 7: 31–32*, **26, 112**

Costly Tower, The, *Luke 14: 28–30*, **71**

Defendant, The, *Matt. 5: 23–26; Luke 12: 57–59*, **32, 61**

Dishonest Steward, The, *Luke 16: 1–8*, **34, 74**

Dragnet, The, *Matt. 13: 47–50*, **51, 64**

Foundations, The, *Matt. 7: 24–27; Luke 6: 46–49*, **99**

Good Samaritan, The, *Luke 10: 29–37*, **7, 17, 20, 91, 96, 97**

Hidden Treasure, The, *Matt. 13: 44*, **70**

Householder, The, *Luke 13: 25–30*, **66**

Invitation to the Banquet (Marriage Feast), The, *Matt. 22: 1–10; Luke 14: 15–24*, **34, 41, 44**

Laborers in the Vineyard, The, *Matt 20: 1–16*, **38, 94**

Last Judgment, The, *Matt. 25: 31–46*, **63, 78**

Leaven, The, *Matt. 13: 33; Luke 13: 20–21*, **48, 64**

Lost Coin, The, *Luke 15: 8–10*, **102**

Lost Sheep, The, *Matt. 18: 12–14; Luke 15: 3–7*, **27, 101**

Marriage Feast, The, *Mark 2: 18–20*, **115**

Mustard Seed, The, *Matt. 13: 31–32; Mark 4: 30–32; Luke 13: 18–19*, **18, 19, 49**

New Wine in Old Wineskins, *Matt. 9: 17; Mark 2: 22; Luke 5: 37–39*, **113**

Pearl of Great Price, The, *Matt. 13: 45–46*, **70, 74**

Persistent Friend, The, *Luke 11: 5–8*, **86**

Pharisee and the Publican, The, *Luke 18: 9–14*, **17, 87, 96**

Places at Table, *Luke 14: 7–10,* **92**

Pounds, The (See The Talents)

Prodigal Son, The, *Luke 15: 11–32,* **17, 40, 102, 111**

Rash King, The, *Luke 14: 31–32,* **72**

Rich Fool, The, *Luke 12: 16–21,* **94**

Rich Man and Lazarus, The, *Luke 16: 19–31,* **17, 108**

Satan Casting Out Satan, *Matt. 12: 25–26; Mark 3: 23–26; Luke 11: 17–18,* **117, 118**

Seed Growing of Itself, The, *Mark 4: 26–29,* **4, 5, 9**

Servant Placed in Authority, The, *Matt. 24: 45–51; Luke 12: 42–48,* **60, 74**

Sower, The, *Matt. 13: 1–23; Mark 4: 1–20; Luke 8: 4–15,* **17, 35, 80**

Strong Man, The, *Matt. 12: 29; Mark 3: 27; Luke 11: 21–22,* **117**

Talents, The, *Matt. 5: 14–30; Luke 19: 11–27,* **17, 34, 75, 77, 79, 92, 94**

Ten Maidens, The, *Matt. 25: 1–13,* **17, 34, 58, 78**

That Which Defiles, *Mark 7: 14–23,* **15, 93**

Treasures New and Old, *Matt. 13: 52,* **115**

Two Debtors, The, *Luke 7: 36–50,* **20, 26, 88, 118**

Two Sons, The, *Matt. 21: 28–31,* **20, 45, 88**

Unclean Spirit, The, *Matt. 12: 43–45; Luke 11: 24–26,* **89, 118**

Unforgiving Servant, The, *Matt. 18: 23–35,* **90, 96**

Unjust Judge, The, *Luke 18: 1–8,* **85**

Unpatched Garment, The, *Matt. 9: 16; Mark 2: 21; Luke 5: 36,* **112**

Unworthy Servant, The, *Luke 17: 7–10,* **91**

Vineyard, The, *Matt. 21: 33–41; Mark 12: 1–12; Luke 20: 9–16,* **17,**

Waiting Servants, The, *Luke 12: 35–38,* **60**

Wedding Garment, The, *Matt. 22: 11–14,* **44**

Wheat and the Tares, The, *Matt. 13: 24–30,* **52**

Biblical Listing of the Parables
(Arranged according to chapter and verse in *Mark, Matthew* and *Luke*. Mark is placed before Matthew because it is usually felt to be the earliest account of the gospel.)

Mark 2: 18–20 The Marriage Feast

Mark 2: 21 The Unpatched Garment (Matt. 9: 16; Luke 5: 36)

Mark 2: 22 New Wine in Old Wineskins (Matt. 9: 17; Luke 5: 37–39)

Mark 3: 23–26 Satan Casting Out Satan (Matt. 12: 25–26; Luke 11: 17–18)

Mark 3: 27 The Strong Man (Matt. 12: 29; Luke 11: 21–22)

Mark 4: 1–20 The Sower (Matt. 13: 1–23; Luke 8: 4–15)

Mark 4: 26–29 The Seed Growing of Itself

Mark 4: 30–32 The Mustard Seed (Matt. 13: 31–32; Luke 13: 18–19)

Mark 7: 14–23 That Which Defiles

Mark 12: 1–12 The Vineyard (Matt. 21: 33–41; Luke 20: 9–16)

Mark 13: 28 The Budding Fig Tree

Matt. 5: 25–26 The Defendant (Luke 12: 57–59)

Matt. 7: 24–27 The Foundations (Luke 6: 47–49)

Matt. 9: 16 (See Mark 2: 21)

Matt. 9: 17 (See Mark 2: 22)

Matt. 11: 16–19 Children in the Market Place (Luke 7: 31–32)

Matt. 12: 25–26 (See Mark 3: 23–26)

Matt. 12: 29 (See Mark 3: 27)

Matt. 12: 43–45 The Unclean Spirit (Luke 11: 24–26)

Matt. 13: 1–23 (See Mark 4: 1–20)

Matt. 13: 24–30 The Wheat and the Tares

Matt. 13: 31–32 (See Mark 4: 30–32)

Matt. 13: 33 The Leaven (Luke 13: 20–21)

Matt. 13: 44 The Hidden Treasure

Matt. 13: 45–46 The Pearl of Great Price

Matt. 13: 47–50 The Dragnet

Matt. 13: 52 Treasures New and Old

Matt. 18: 12–14 The Lost Sheep (Luke 15: 3–7)

Matt. 18: 23–35 The Unforgiving Servant

Matt. 20: 1–16 The Laborers in the Vineyard

Matt. 21: 28–31 The Two Sons

Matt. 21: 33–41 (See Mark 12: 1–12)

Matt. 22: 1–10 The Invitation to the Banquet (Marriage Feast) (Luke 14: 15–24)

Matt. 22: 11–14 The Wedding Garment

Matt. 24: 32 (See Mark 13: 28)

Matt. 24: 43–44 The Burglar

Matt. 24: 45–51 The Servant Placed in Authority (Luke 12: 42–48)

Matt. 25: 1–13 The Ten Maidens

Matt. 25: 14–30 The Talents

Matt. 25: 31–46 The Last Judgment

Luke 5: 36 (See Mark 2: 21)

Luke 5: 37–39 (See Mark 2: 22)

Luke 6: 47–49 (See Matt. 7: 24–27)

Luke 7: 36–50 The Two Debtors

Luke 7: 31–32 (See Matt. 11: 16–19)

Luke 8: 4–15 (See Mark 4: 1–20)

Luke 10: 29–37 The Good Samaritan

Luke 11: 5–8 The Persistent Friend

Luke 11: 17–18 (See Mark 3: 23–26)

Luke 11: 21–22 (See Mark 3: 27)

Luke 11: 24–26 (See Matt. 12: 43–45)

Luke 12: 16–21 The Rich Fool

Luke 12: 35–38 The Waiting Servants

Luke 12: 39–40 (See Matt. 24: 43–44)

Luke 12: 42–48 (See Matt. 24: 45–51)

Luke 12: 57–59 (See Matt. 5: 25–26)

Luke 13: 6–9 The Barren Fig Tree

Luke 13: 18–19 (See Mark 4: 30–32)

Luke 13: 20–21 (See Matt. 13: 33)
Luke 13: 25–30 The Householder
Luke 14: 7–10 Places at Table
Luke 14: 15–24 (See Matt. 22: 1–10)
Luke 14: 28–30 The Costly Tower
Luke 14: 31–32 The Rash King
Luke 15: 3–7 (See Matt. 18: 12–14)
Luke 15: 8–10 The Lost Coin
Luke 15: 11–32 The Prodigal Son
Luke 16: 1–8 The Dishonest Steward
Luke 16: 19–31 The Rich Man and Lazarus
Luke 17: 7–10 The Unworthy Servant
Luke 18: 1–8 The Unjust Judge
Luke 18: 9–14 The Pharisee and the Publican
Luke 19: 11–27 (See Matt. 25: 14–30)
Luke 20: 9–16 (See Mark 12: 1–12)